craft **workshop**

# batik

craft **workshop**

# batik

the art of fabric decorating and painting in over 20 beautiful projects

# Susie Stokoe

photography by Nicki Dowey

southwater

This edition is published by Southwater

Southwater is an imprint of Anness Publishing Ltd
Hermes House, 88–89 Blackfriars Road, London SE1 8HA
tel. 020 7401 2077; fax 020 7633 9499
www.southwaterbooks.com; info@anness.com

© Anness Publishing Ltd 2000, 2004

UK agent: The Manning Partnership Ltd, 6 The Old Dairy,
Melcombe Road, Bath BA2 3LR; tel. 01225 478444;
fax 01225 478440; sales@manning-partnership.co.uk

UK distributor: Grantham Book Services Ltd, Isaac Newton
Way, Alma Park Industrial Estate, Grantham, Lincs NG31 9SD;
tel. 01476 541080; fax 01476 541061; orders@gbs.tbs-ltd.co.uk

North American agent/distributor: National Book Network,
4501 Forbes Boulevard, Suite 200, Lanham, MD 20706;
tel. 301 459 3366; fax 301 429 5746; www.nbnbooks.com

Australian agent/distributor: Pan Macmillan Australia, Level
18, St Martins Tower, 31 Market St, Sydney, NSW 2000;
tel. 1300 135 113; fax 1300 135 103;
customer.service@macmillan.com.au

New Zealand agent/distributor: David Bateman Ltd,
30 Tarndale Grove, Off Bush Road, Albany, Auckland;
tel. (09) 415 7664; fax (09) 415 8892

A CIP catalogue record for this book is available from the
British Library.

Publisher: Joanna Lorenz
Senior Editor: Doreen Gillon
Editor: Heather Dewhurst
Editorial Reader: Joy Wotton
Designer: Lilian Lindblom
Photographer: Nicki Dowey
Contributors: Helen Heery, Sipra Majumder
Illustrators: Madeleine David, Robert Highton
Production Controller: Joanna King

Previously published as *Practical Batik*

10 9 8 7 6 5 4 3 2 1

NOTE
The author has made every effort to ensure that all
the instructions in this book are accurate and safe,
and therefore cannot accept liability for any resulting
injury, damage or loss to persons or property
however it may arise.

# Contents

# INTRODUCTION

THE FREEDOM AND IMMEDIACY OF WORKING WITH DYE AND FABRIC IS SIMILAR TO THAT OF WATERCOLOUR PAINTING. BATIK IS AN ANCIENT CRAFT USING WAX AND DYE AND THE EFFECTS THAT CAN BE ACHIEVED THROUGH RESIST DYEING CAN OFTEN RESULT IN UNPREDICTABLE TEXTURES. THIS MEANS THAT NO PARTICULAR PIECE CAN BE COPIED EXACTLY. OVER THE CENTURIES, THIS HAS ONLY SERVED TO HEIGHTEN PEOPLE'S FASCINATION WITH THE TECHNIQUE.

BATIK DESIGNS CAN BE AS COMPLICATED OR AS SIMPLE AS THE CRAFTSPERSON DESIRES. THEY CAN BE REALISTIC AND PICTORIAL OR PURELY EXPRESSIVE. STRONG CONTRASTING COLOURS CAN BE USED TO PRODUCE DRAMATIC CONTEMPORARY DESIGNS. THE LUSTRE OF SILKS ADDS A BRILLIANCE TO DYE COLOURS, PRODUCING AN ALMOST LUMINOUS QUALITY. THE MAIN INCENTIVE WHEN UNDERTAKING A BATIK PROJECT IS TO ENJOY THE MEDIUM, SO ALLOW THE VERSATILITY OF THE WAX AND DYE TO REVEAL ITSELF GRADUALLY TO YOU. EXPERIMENT AT EVERY OPPORTUNITY YOU CAN WITH DIFFERENT TEXTURES AND TECHNIQUES.

*Left: All sorts of materials, including silk, velvet and leather, can be decorated using this versatile method of dyeing.*

# HISTORY OF BATIK

Over the centuries, the decoration of textiles has become highly skilled and has reached great heights of complexity and sophistication. Batik dyeing is an ancient craft whose most distinctive feature today is the cracks or tiny vein-like lines, which appear when the wax cracks before dyeing. Traditionally, this was seen as imperfection, but it can also be used to create interesting decorative effects.

The technique of batik and resist dyeing varies slightly around the world, although the principle remains the same: that water and wax (resist) repel each other. Therefore, wax-covered areas of fabric will be unable to accept dye. Wax, rice paste and mud have all been used as types of resist. The application of these mediums can vary widely from freehand, using paper cones or the pen-like canting, to repeated designs achieved by using wooden stamps, copper Cap blocks, fine paper or wooden stencils. The possibilities and variations are limitless.

The word "batik" occurred for the first time in Dutch texts of the 17th century, although the word is probably Indonesian in origin; the Indonesian word "tik" means a drop. In Javanese, batik is known as "Ambatik", meaning drawing and writing. Although drawings from India appear to make reference to garments that could have been batik, there have been no actual discoveries of early cloth. In fact the earliest validated examples come from Egypt and date back to the 5th century AD.

Other early examples of batik include a set of screens dating back to the Japanese Nara period (AD 646–794). These screens were thought to have been decorated by Chinese artists working as emigrants in Japan or thousands of miles away in their homeland.

*Right: This beautiful, intricate batik cotton fabric with its repeated patterns and delicate detail is from Cirebon, Java. It is an excellent example of 20th-century Kratonan-style batik. Courtesy of the Trustees of the V&A.*

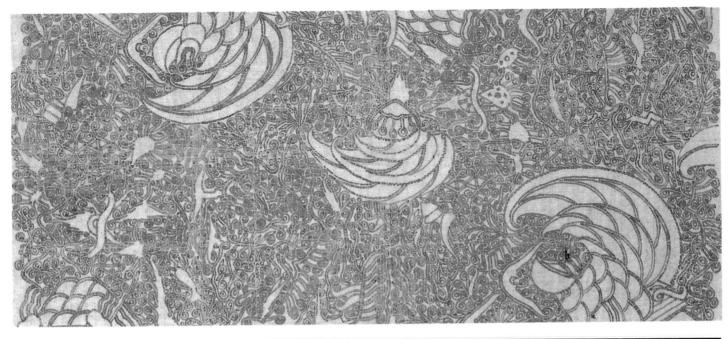

The art of decorating textiles with natural colorants or dyes has been practised for many centuries. The earliest recorded use of dyes can be found in ancient Chinese writings of 2500 BC. The cultivation of silk is also widely accredited to the Chinese (although it may have been produced in India as early as 1000 BC). Batik was certainly practised in China during the Sui dynasty (AD 710–794) and while there is some dispute over batik's true origins, there is a general consensus that batik should be attributed to China and travelled from country to country along with the export of silk. Silk was a highly prized cloth and was exported from China to Japan, Central Asia and then to the Middle East and India. This trading route is known today as the silk route. By

*Above: This is a 20th century waxed cotton batik sample from Java. Courtesy of the Trustees of the V&A.*

*Right: Four Balinese girls holding decorated and intricate batik designs, with other batiked fabric stacked on their heads.*

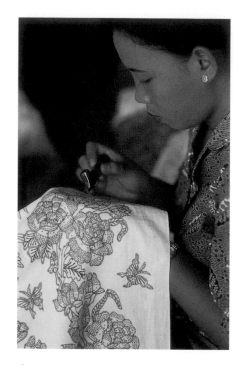

*Above: A young woman in Indonesia using a canting (sometimes this is called a tjanting) to create a batik design on fabric.*

*Right: A traditional batik design from central Java.*

1677 there is also evidence that trading continued from India to Java and Persia.

Japan was highly influenced by the Chinese Sui and T'ang dynasties and it is possible that early batiks were exported from China to Japan. These could well include a set of screens dating back to the Japanese Nara period (646–794 AD). In Japan, during the 8th century AD, batik, or Roketsu-zome, using liquid wax was a common way of decorating cloth. Japan is well known for its wonderful textiles, especially the rich decoration used on kimonos (translated as "the thing worn") of the Edo period (AD 1600–1868).

With numerous daily activities requiring kneeling or cross-legged sitting positions, the Japanese needed clothing that was unrestrictive. This, coupled with a general lack of interest in displaying the human figure, meant that decoration became all-important, often used to display social position, profession or occasion.

Resist dyeing, or Chaya-zome, in Japan was often mixed with other dyeing techniques such as tie dye to create highly complex patterns. The technique was further refined using rice paste as the resist. This was applied to the cloth through paper or fine wooden stencils. At the beginning of the 18th century, Miyazaki Yûzen refined this method even further creating the distinctive Yuzen style of stencil and resist dyeing. These designs normally have the rich decoration contained in well-defined areas.

Rice paste was also drawn on to the cloth through fine paper cones, making the designs more fluid and giving the artist more freedom.

The country which has developed batik to the greatest heights of complexity and sophistication is Java. Batik was exported from India to Java, which is why the most common fabric used for batik production in Java is cotton. The technique and design tradition reflect the culture and religion of the country. Java's main batik centres are Yogyakarta, Solo, Cirebon, Pekalongan, Tegal Taksimalaya, Indramayu, Garut, Lesam and Semarang.

Batik was formerly the fabric worn by the aristocracy, who having the time and considered to possess a gentle hand, would do the decoration themselves, producing elaborate and valuable cloths. This, in turn, led to servants of aristocratic households becoming involved in batik production. Finally, it became the national costume.

In central Java, traditional freehand or geometric designs and techniques are passed down through generations with each family of patterns given names such as Ceplokan, which are repetitive designs, or Kawung, which are circular designs. Colours in central Java tend to be more sombre than on the north coast, which had a more commercial attitude to design.

Northern Java was influenced by Arabian and Chinese merchants coming across the sea. Traditional designs were adapted to suit potential buyers. Chinese influences can be seen in the use of brighter colours, such as pink, yellow and blue, and in the array of filigree-like birds, flowers and border patterns.

The introduction of Islam, which forbade the life-like depiction of human and animal forms, led to even more stylized patterns and the use of green, which is a sacred colour in the Muslim world. Dutch and Eurasian buyers were influenced by European designs and

wanted floral bouquets, butterflies and birds. The Governor General of Java, Sir Thomas Raffles, produced a book on the history of batik that increased interest in the technique in Europe.

In 1835 a factory was set up in Leyden, Holland, to produce batik commercially. Factories followed in Rotterdam, Appledorn, Helmuand and Haarlem. To make batik a commercial success in Europe, new techniques were developed as it was difficult to replicate at low cost the complex designs from Java. The Dutch employed Indonesian craftsman to teach the skill to Dutch workers who, in turn, set up workshops in Java. These workshops developed a technique called "Cap", a method of block printing wax, therefore making batik cheaper to produce. The Cap block is made by soldering fine copper wire

and pins into an elaborate pattern. The blocks fit together to form an all-over repeating design.

After the general economic collapse of the 1920s, batik again became a technique used by individual artists and craftsmen. A school of batik was opened in Holland, and batik became an accepted element of arts and crafts. The often intricate and stylized decoration was a contributing influence to the Art Nouveau style and to artists such as Madame Pangon, Chris Lebeau and Charles Rennie Mackintosh.

*Above: Batik-style textile designs started to become popular in Europe throughout the 19th century. This piece was made in France in 1888 by using rollers and blocks on cotton.*

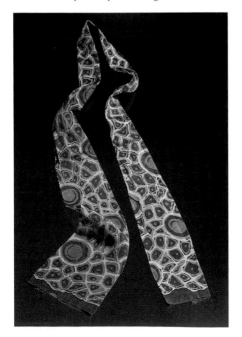

*Left: A batik-printed silk tie, with Art Nouveau influences, by Ilse von Scheel, Germany, 1913–14. Courtesy of the Trustees of the V&A. Sara Hodges.*

# GALLERY

Batik is a traditional method of decorating fabric. However, it can also be highly inventive way of applying colour to many surfaces, not just textiles — you can experiment on other materials such as paper, wood, leather and plastic. Contemporary craftspeople experiment with batik and re-invent the technique by combining old techniques with new ideas and materials to develop original and inspiring work.

*Above:* EDGE
A cotton batik, wax resist, reactive and discharged and dyed, 1993. 127 x 94 cm (50 x 37½ in).
NOEL DYRENFORTH

*Right:* PINK MARBLE
A silk and velvet viscose wrap, which uses the technique of cracking to create the design. White velvet is dyed pale pink, and large areas are then waxed. It is dip-dyed in dark pink, which cracks the wax. It is then waxed again and dip-dyed in indigo, resulting in further cracking. The texture of the cracking complements that of the velvet.
HELEN HEERY

*Left:* SNOWFLAKE &
STARFLOWER
CUSHIONS
Batik nature studies in fine
cotton lawn pieced with
Irish linen. The images are
handpainted wax resist
using various hog brushes,
plus dipped cardboard
strips and scrunched
papers to create lines and
textures.
ALISON TILLEY

*Below:* FIVE
A silk batik on several
pieces of plastic backing –
wax resist, reactive dyed
and etched, 1999. NOEL
DYRENFORTH

*Below left:* ADRIFT
A cotton batik – wax
resist, hand painted and
discharge dyed, 1998.
144 x 162 cm (57½ x 65 in).
NOEL DYRENFORTH

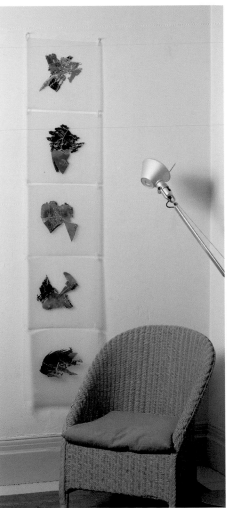

*Left:* MONDAY MONDAY
A batik which was wax-resisted repeatedly using a canting and brushes. It was then dip-dyed in a succession of reactive dyes, starting with a light colour and finishing with a dark one.
ROSI ROBINSON

*Left:* CATCH A FALLING STAR
Layers of black tissue paper, paraffin wax resist, bleached and dyed over coloured images on newsprint. The torn away tissue papers reveals underlaying colours, structures and forms. Batik on paper, 80 x 90 cm (31½ x 36 in).
HETTY VAN BOEKHOUT

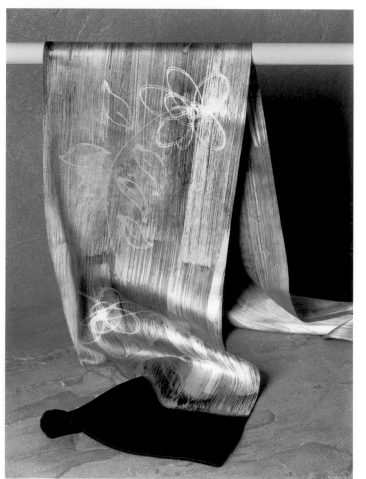

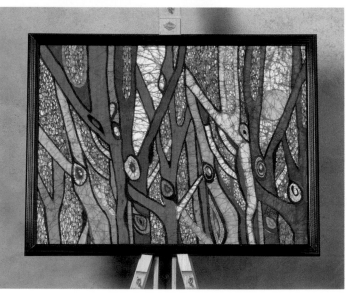

*Left:* STRATA
A crêpe satin scarf. A flower and stem were waxed using a canting before dyeing different areas pale blue and cream. Using a wide brush, large areas were waxed so that the brush stroke can be seen. It was re-dyed gold, brown, and blue and re-waxed before dip-dyeing in indigo. HELEN HEERY

*Above:* WOODLAND
A traditional batik design on cotton fabric. Beeswax and paraffin were used to achieve the crackle effect.
SIPRA MAJUMDER

*Left:* STAITHES AFTERNOON

For this batik, wax was applied to fine cotton using various bristle brushes, after an initial pencil sketch. Many successive colours were used, by the traditional dye bath method, to capture the effect of light on water.
HEATHER GATT

*Below:* ORNAMENTAL

This batik uses tissue paper on chinese paper, paraffin wax resist, procion dye and bleach. Overlapping transparent tissue paper creates a collage: a controlled and complex pattern of colours and forms. Batik on paper 80 x 75 cm (31½ x 29½ in).
HETTY VAN BOEKHOUT

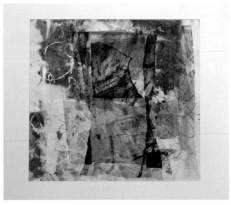

*Far left:* KUBLA KHAN

A batik wall hanging on light calico. It is part of a triptych. Wax was applied with a brush and canting, whilst light, airy colours were achieved by using transparent acrylic inks in conjunction with traditional dyes and gold fabric paint.
HEATHER GATT

*Left:* LOOP

A scuptural piece of wood veneer decorated with batik and wax resist dyed, 1996. 90 x 50 x 30 cm (36 x 20 x 12 in).
NOEL DYRENFORTH

# MATERIALS

When preparing batik, it is easy to become confused with the huge variety of natural and manufactured dyes available. Always check the manufacturer's instructions to find out how to dilute and fix the dye. Be sure to check out how your dye will react on a small sample piece of material. You should bear in mind how the colours will alter after repeated dyeings.

**Dyes** can be used either in a dye bath or painted in concentrated form directly on to the fabric surface. Direct or application dyes have a good range of colours. They are intermixable and soluble in water, though, after mixing, the dye bath should be allowed to cool for work with batik to avoid melting the wax.

For painting directly on to cloth, there is now a variety of easy-to-use dyes and fabric paints, many of which are developed with the craft dyer in mind. Use the semi-transparent dyes, such as the silk paints that do not contain binders, as these give beautiful, clear, translucent colours. Most of these can be dry-cleaned and are set by ironing.

**Reactive dyes** are so-called because of the presence of an alkali or soda in the dye that sticks to the cloth fibres. If the alkali is not present, the dye will wash out. After the alkali has been added, these dyes only have a life span of about four hours, but they have a range of strong colours and a good degree of fastness.

**Salt** gives dramatic effects when dropped on to damp silk paints. The salt draws the dye into it, leaving dark lines and spots on the surface of the cloth. Rock salts give craggy lines, while salt grains give a more speckled effect. Make sure the silk is dry before removing the salt, which may take 20 minutes. Salt is also used with cold water and direct dyes as a fixative.

**Tissue paper** This can be resist painted or dyed using wax.

**Japanese paper** is a suitable surface on which to batik. Papers with unusual textures will give different effects. (See Fabrics for more information.)

**Brown paper** is used to iron out wax. Newspaper or lining paper can be used.

**Mylar film** is used to cut stencils from. It is better than stencil card as the non-porous plastic surface allows one to peel off hardened wax after use.

**Tracing paper** is used to transfer designs on to cloth or other materials.

**Sewing materials** such as a needle and thread will be needed for finishing projects and hemming. In some cases, a sewing machine may be useful.

**Dressmaker's pins** will be needed for finishing edges and hems. When working with very fine silk use fine pins so as not to pull or damage the silk.

**Sponges** are ideal for covering large areas of material with dye.

**Rags** Always have a good supply of rags around when you are working. They can be used to wipe the canting as molten wax on the exterior of the canting may get smudged on to the cloth. It is also a good idea to protect areas of your work when you are working, especially when wax drops fall between the wax pot and the area you are working on. Errant drops of wax falling on cloth are difficult to remove.

**Clear gum** is used instead of wax for batik on leather.

**Wax** An all-purpose batik wax consisting of paraffin and microcrystalline waxes is sold in granulated form. Some suppliers will supply these ready mixed; however, if you want to prepare your own wax for batik, here are some recipes to try.

- *Strong wax (for canting)*
  - 6 parts pine resin
  - 4 parts paraffin wax
  - 1 part beeswax
  - 0.25 parts damor gum
  - 0.25 parts fat
- *Blocking wax (for covering large areas)*
  - 2 parts beeswax
  - 1 part pine resin
  - 0.5 parts damor gum
  - 0.5 parts microcrystalline wax
  - 0.1 parts fat
- *Crackle wax (for cracking or marble effect)*
  - 5 parts paraffin wax
  - 5 parts pine resin
  - 1 part damor gum
  - 0.2 parts fat

KEY

1 Reactive dyes
2 Silk paints
3 Water soluble glue
4 Leather dyes
5 Sewing materials
6 Pins
7 Fabrics
8 Sponge
9 Wax
10 Salt
11 Tracing paper
12 Brown paper
13 Mylar film
14 Japanese paper
15 Tissue paper

# EQUIPMENT

A THERMOSTATICALLY CONTROLLED WAX POT OR ELECTRIC SAUCEPAN IS THE IDEAL PIECE OF EQUIPMENT FOR HEATING WAX. WHEN STARTING OUT WITH BATIK, A DOUBLE BOILER AND A KITCHEN THERMOMETER TO CHECK THE TEMPERATURE WILL BE PERFECTLY ADEQUATE. YOU MAY WANT TO INVEST IN SPECIAL EQUIPMENT IF YOU DECIDE TO DO A LOT OF BATIK WORK. THIS IS AVAILABLE FROM MOST GOOD CRAFT STORES.

**Masking tape** is useful to tape down fabric while you work on it. It also protects silk frames from becoming marked with dye.

**Double-sided tape** is used to secure cloth or paper.

**Fabric scissors** Some fabric can be quite difficult to cut, so have a pair of sharp fabric scissors to make a nice, clean edge. Blunt scissors may cause lightweight cloth such as silk to tear or pull.

**Paper scissors** are useful for cutting out designs. Never cut paper with fabric scissors as this will make them blunt.

**Ruler and set (T) square** Used when drawing up a design to scale or trimming down cloth so that it is square. When you are cutting down designs with a craft knife, it is best to use a ruler with a metal edge.

**Tape measure** Use a tape measure to measure lengths of cloth or frame sizes.

**Dressmaker's water-soluble pen** This pen is useful when drawing a design on to cloth as the pen marks are easily removed with a light spray of water. Remember, however, that dye will also remove these pen marks so they are only really suitable for drawing areas to be waxed; for other areas of the design use a soft pencil.

**Shallow dye bath** Industrial-sized catering trays are good for this; use either plastic or metal. Etching baths will suffice. It is important to keep the batik flat while dyeing to prevent unwanted cracks appearing in the wax.

**Thermostatically controlled wax-pot or double boiler** Wax pots are specially designed to heat wax to a constant temperature. You can also use a double boiler or saucepan and pan.

**Gas or electric ring burner** When you are using a double boiler to heat wax, it is best to use a gas or electric ring burner rather than the hob (stove) as the molten wax needs to be near the piece of work.

**Canting** A tool used for drawing with hot wax. sometimes called a *tjanting*. The shape of the canting may vary according to where in the world it comes from. It is similar to a pen and it is useful when drawing fine designs. Cantings can have varying width spouts giving different line qualities, and with several spouts allowing one to draw parallel lines. Electric cantings are available, which keep the wax hot.

**Brushes** For batik, you will need a good selection of brushes. To apply dye, you will need soft natural fibre brushes or sponge brushes for large areas. More substantial brushes will be needed for applying wax, such as those used for oil painting. Before you start, experiment with the effects of different brushes, or try other tools such as combs, toothbrushes or sponges.

**Silk painting frames** are sold in various sizes including adjustable, which is the most useful. For particularly large batiks you may need to make your own frame.

**Silk pins** are fine-pointed, flat-headed pins with three points that are easy to remove and they ensure that the silk is not pulled or torn. You can also use fine-pointed push pins or drawing pins.

**Staple guns** can be used to secure a finished batik to a stretcher or frame so that it can be hung on the wall.

**Rubber or latex gloves** should be used when working with a dye bath to prevent dyeing your hands.

**Thermometers** are needed when doing batik to keep the wax at a constant temperature of 120°C (248°F).

**Pallet** China pallettes are ideal for mixing silk paints but egg cups or plates can also be used. Try to avoid plastic pallets as silk paints will usually stain these quite heavily.

**Measuring jug (cup)** Exact quantities of water may need to be measured when you are preparing a dye bath.

**Wool dauber** This is used to batik leather.

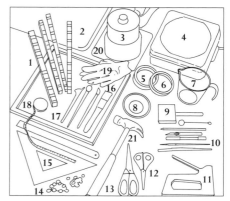

KEY

| | |
|---|---|
| 1 Silk-painting frames | 11 Staple gun |
| 2 Shallow dye bath | 12 Paper scissors |
| 3 Double boiler | 13 Fabric scissors |
| 4 Electric ring | 14 Silk pins |
| 5 Masking tape | 15 Ruler and set (T) square |
| 6 Double-sided tape | 16 Brush |
| 7 Measuring jug | 17 Cantings |
| 8 Pallette | 18 Tape measure |
| 9 Wool dauber | 19 Latex gloves |
| 10 Dressmaker's water soluble pen | 20 Cork mat |
| | 21 Hammer |

# FABRIC

It is important to consider carefully the type of fabric you are using before starting a project. For best results with batik and home dyeing use natural fibres such as silk, cotton and linen. Viscose rayon is the only man-made fibre suitable for batik. You can batik almost any natural porous surface, such as cotton, silk, linen, leather, paper and wood.

Always check the manufacturer's instructions for fabric recommendations and guidelines as to washing temperatures and colour fastness. When you buy fabric, it will normally have a certain amount of dressing or finish on it left over from manufacture. In order for wax and dyes to penetrate sufficiently, this should be removed by washing. Special dyes have been developed for leather and silk.

**Silk** is one of the strongest textile fibres, although it still has a wonderful, luxurious quality. Silk is easy to dye, and there are a whole range of dyes and fabric paints developed solely for use on silk. Silk fabric types vary in weight and different textures, from rough wild silks such as tussah, to strong hard-wearing twills, which are recognizable by the tiny diagonal rib in the weave. Smooth high shine satin has a luxurious quality and is good for special items such as scarves.
**Crêpe de Chine** is a delicate lightweight cloth and should be treated with the greatest of care. The characteristic surface texture is a result of highly-twisted yarns being used in the manufacture. The fine delicate nature of this fabric makes it ideal for special items.
**Pongee Silk** is sold in many different weights ranging from No.5 to No.10; the higher the number, the heavier it is. This silk can also be called habutai or Japanese silk and is often used for lining. It has a nice smooth finish with a soft sheen and it is ideal for batik and most silk painting techniques.

**Wild silk** has a wonderful exotic feel and texture and is readily available in a wide variety of weights and colours including two-tone. Some of the wild or raw silks such as tussah have an almost bark-like texture. The wild tussah silk moth produces a silk that is often uneven and causes slubs in the woven cloth. The texture of these cloths can prove a problem with batik as the wax may not penetrate the cloth, and when working with the direct dyeing method you may find that colours bleed into each other; this effect could however be worked into a design. Doupion silks have less of a slub as the once wild Bombix-mori moth that produces the silk has now been cultivated, though you may still find that wax does not penetrate the fabric entirely.
**Cotton** is produced from the *Gossypium* shrub and is available in a wide range of weights. It is easy to dye and gives a good strong colour. It is a strong durable fabric that can be used for all home furnishing projects. Always test your chosen fabric with your dye type and consider the most suitable weight for your project. Light-weight cottons with a smooth surface such as lawn, poplin, satin and organdie are most suitable for batik. Ask your fabric supplier for advice on washing temperatures.
**Linen** is produced from the fibres of the flax plant. In comparison with cotton the weave of linen is more irregular, which can prove a problem with batik, although the cloth has a wonderful dry natural look and is suitable with most dye types. It comes in various weights from dress

weight to heavy canvas, and is often mixed with other yarn types such as silk or viscose; these will also dye, though in the case of viscose you may achieve paler results. Fine, flexible high-quality linens such as the ones produced in Ireland are the best for batik. Again, ask your fabric supplier for washing advice and experiment with your dye type before starting.
**Velvet** The most suitable velvet to use for batik and home dyeing is made from a silk and viscose mix (this velvet is also suitable for devoré). This cloth has a fluid quality with wonderful drape, but it can be expensive so it is best used for special items or garments. It will readily accept dye, giving rich and intense colours.
**Paper** is a porous material and is suitable for batik. Hand-made papers with rich textures can add another dimension to your batik. When working with paper, most of the wax can be removed by ironing, but final grease marks and wax residue will leave dark marks on the design. As paper cannot be washed, it is a good idea to entirely cover the batik with wax before ironing in order to hide these marks.
**Leather** The technique of batik can be used on leather using a water soluble glue or gum instead of wax. Many household glues when dry have a rubbery quality and can easily be peeled off the surface of the leather. Their gum-like quality will adhere them sufficiently to the leather and act as a suitable resist to the dye. Do not use wax on leather as it stains. Special dyes and finishing treatments have been developed for leather that give strong fast colours.

**Caring for Silk** Silk should be washed by hand with mild liquid detergents, or natural or olive oil soaps. Always try to avoid crushing or wringing the cloth especially with satins as this may damage the surface of the cloth. Silk should be dried slowly by hanging it flat from a line. Excess water can be removed by rolling the cloth in a towel. Silk should be pressed on the wrong side while still damp. Silk should never be boil-washed, so always use dyes that can be dry-cleaned in order that the wax and grease marks can be completely removed.

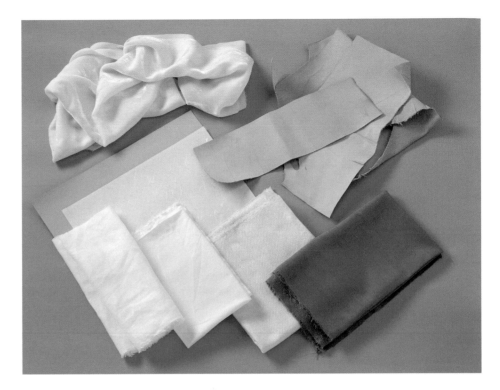

KEY
1 Silk
2 Leather
3 Wild silk
4 Cotton
5 Linen
6 Paper
7 Velvet

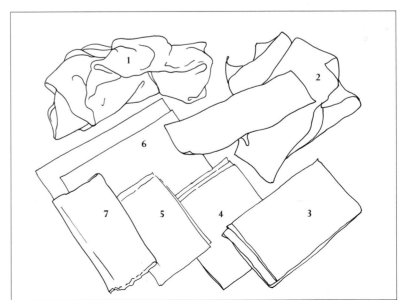

# BASIC TECHNIQUES

A FEW SIMPLE TECHNIQUES, ONCE MASTERED, WILL ENABLE YOU TO FULLY EXPLORE THE ART OF BATIK. THE PROJECTS IN THIS BOOK ARE DESIGNED TO USE SOME OR ALL OF THESE BASIC TECHNIQUES, AND THEY WILL HELP TO FURTHER HONE YOUR SKILL AND UNDERSTANDING OF THE MEDIUM.

THE BASIC PRINCIPLES AND TECHNIQUES OF RESIST DYEING AND BATIK NEVER CHANGE, ALTHOUGH BY PRACTISING, YOUR SKILLS WILL INCREASE, ALLOWING YOU TO ADD IN LAYERS OF COLOUR, INCREASE YOUR ARTISTIC ABILITY AND ACHIEVE MUCH MORE COMPLEX RESULTS.

### MAKING A BASIC FRAME

The majority of good craft retailers will stock a range of silk-painting frames, the adjustable ones being the most useful. Embroidery frames (hoops) can be used when working with small areas but for large pieces it may be necessary to make your own frame. When making a frame, always make sure the inside edge of the frame is at least 2 cm (¾ in) larger than the size you want your finished piece of batik to be. This will allow for wastage or enable you to trim away untidy edges.

1 Cut four pieces of planed wood to the size you want your frame to be. Using wood adhesive, glue two pieces together to make a right angle. Then glue the remaining two pieces in the same way.

3 Glue the two right angles together to make the frame. Nail the panel pins (brads) into each corner to make the frame firm. Sand down any rough pieces of wood so that they are free of splinters.

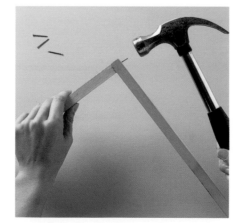

2 When the glue is set, tap one or two panel pins (brads) into the corner joint to hold it firmly.

4 Protect the frame from dye by covering it in masking tape before pinning on your cloth.

## PINNING SILK TO A FRAME

It is possible to apply wax to a cloth on a non-porous surface, such as metal or plastic, to which the wax will not stick. However, when applying dye, a frame is most commonly used to support the fabric, keeping it suspended above the work surface. This eliminates the possibility of any seepage through the material that could result in the dye smudging or being unevenly distributed.

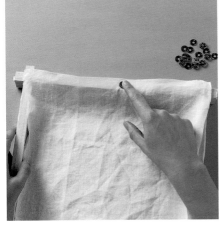

1 Select a frame with a window (the inside area) that is at least 2 cm (¾ in) larger than the size you want your finished batik to be (this allows you to trim away untidy edges once you have completed this project). Cut down a piece of cloth to the size of your frame and place your first silk pin in the centre of the furthest edge.

2 Working out from the central pin towards each corner, continue placing the pins an equal distance apart. Make sure that the fabric is pulled taut.

3 When you have completed this side, begin pinning the opposite side. Pull the fabric across the frame, placing the pins opposite to those on the first side, once again pulling the fabric taut.

4 Pin down one of the remaining two sides and then the final side, again pulling the fabric across the frame, placing the pins opposite each other. When pinned, the cloth should be springy to the touch. Do not pull the cloth too tight as it may tear around the pins.

## USING A DYE BATH

This technique is the more traditional method of batik, and it is best used when large areas of flat colour need to be achieved. When using a dye bath for batik, it is imperative that you use a cold water dye so as not to affect the consistency of the wax. It is also important to keep waxed areas of cloth flat while submerged in the dye to prevent unwanted cracks appearing in the wax. However, it is inevitable that some cracking will occur, especially when working on pieces with large areas of wax. The veining that is produced by cracking is evidence of this method of batik and has become an extremely effective technique in itself. (See Cracking.)

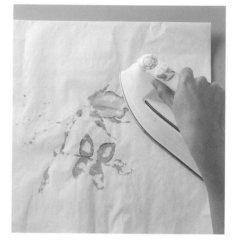

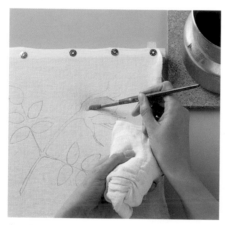

1 Place the design under the fabric and trace it on to the cloth with a pencil. To prevent the fabric from moving, stick it to the work surface with masking tape. Pin the fabric to the painting frame. Heat the wax to a steady 120°C (248°F) and fill in the flower petals with wax using a brush. Check the back of the cloth to see if the wax has penetrated sufficiently. The cloth should appear semi-transparent when waxed. If areas of the cloth remain opaque, reapply the molten wax on the back.

2 Mix up a dye bath with a cold water dye (green), carefully following the dye manufacturer's instructions. Remove the cloth from the frame. Dampen the waxed cloth and place it in the dye bath, keeping the waxed area as flat as possible. When the desired colour has been achieved, remove the fabric from the bath and rinse it in cold water. Unless cracking is required, be careful not to fold or crease the fabric while rinsing. Hang it up to dry.

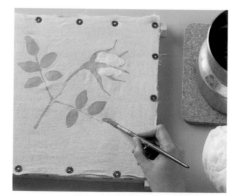

3 When the cloth is dry, re-pin the cloth on to the frame and fill in the leaves and stem with molten wax. Check the back again to make sure that the wax has penetrated sufficiently.

4 Prepare your second dye bath (blue). Again, be careful not to fold or crease the waxed areas while in the dye bath. After dyeing, rinse the cloth in cold water. This piece will not be re-dyed, so it no longer matters if the cloth is creased. Finally, remove the wax by ironing the cloth between pieces of newsprint, brown or lining paper (see Finishing).

5 You can continue waxing and dyeing to build up more layers of colour and detail. However, most dyes suitable for dye baths can only be overlaid about three times. After this, they no longer "take" to the cloth and they cease to be colour-fast.

## DIRECT DYEING

The basic principle of this technique is to use the wax as a boundary. As with a stained-glass window, where one colour is separated from another by a line of lead, this technique of batik separates one colour from another by a line of wax. It is imperative that the lines of wax have no breaks, as breaks would will allow one block of colour to bleed into the next. By painting the dye on to the cloth, one can achieve similar effects to that of water-colour painting by blending colours.

1 Place the design underneath the fabric and trace it on to the cloth using a soft pencil. If necessary, stick the cloth to the work surface using masking tape to prevent it from moving. Pin the fabric to a frame. Heat the wax in a wax pot or double boiler to a steady 120°C (248°F). Using a canting, draw in the outline of the flower petals with molten wax. When the wax is applied, the fabric should become semi-transparent. If the wax has not penetrated the fibres sufficiently, the fabric will remain opaque. Check the back of the fabric for breaks in the wax outline and fill them in by waxing on the back.

2 Using a green fabric dye (transparent dyes not containing binders are ideal), fill in the entire background to the flower shape with a brush. Work quickly to ensure an even colour. If you choose to use a thick fabric paint, be sure to dilute it to the consistency of ink.

3 Draw in the outline of the leaves and flower stem with the molten wax. Check the back of the fabric again to make sure that the wax has penetrated sufficiently.

4 Take a blue fabric dye and fill in the background to the flower with a brush. Further applications of dye can be made on the remaining non-waxed areas of the cloth. For example, in this project the flower area was left white to allow the application of a pink dye, but you could easily do the same for the stems and leaves. With this technique, you decide how many different colours you use.

5 Apply pink dye over the flower petals. Remove the wax (see Finishing). Waxing and dyeing can continue indefinitely or until the entire cloth is covered in wax. It is often the case that this method is used to add detail to a piece that was started using the dye bath method of batik.

## BATIK USING A STENCIL

Stencils can be used in batik either to replicate a specific design or to protect the remainder of your work while you add texture to an area (that is, you employ more wax or dye). In this example, the wax is splashed on the surface. You may, however, wish to use a crumpled rag or stipple brush to apply the wax. Here we have chosen to use a direct dyeing method, although a dye bath could also be used when working on larger pieces.

1 Pin the fabric to a frame. Heat the wax in a wax pot or double boiler to a steady 120°C (248°F). Using a fine artist's brush or canting, wax around the inside edge of the frame. This will control the bleed of the dye and keep your work neat.

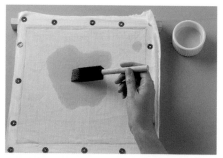

2 Using an artist's brush or sponge, fill in the square with the palest colour (yellow). Allow the dye to bleed from the painting tool towards the wax outline rather than overloading the cloth with dye.

3 Draw a pear shape on to a piece of Mylar film and cut it out using a craft knife. Place this stencil in the centre. Cover all exposed cloth around the stencil with scrap paper. Using a medium brush, flick molten wax on to the exposed cloth inside the stencil. Remove the stencil before the wax is completely set.

4 Again using a large brush or sponge, paint the square of cloth with your second colour (red), going over the waxed area. When the fabric is dry, replace the stencil and flick more wax and again over-paint with your third and darkest colour (brown).

5 Pick off all excess wax. Remove the fabric from the frame and iron it between pieces of newsprint, brown or lining paper to remove all remaining wax. With this technique, the process of waxing and dyeing can be repeated as long as there are still exposed areas of cloth within the stencil shape.

## FINISHING

You must remove all wax from a finished piece of batik to restore the fabric's drape. Ironing will remove most of the wax, but it will be necessary to boil or dry-clean the fabric to remove final grease marks and wax residue. Silks should not be boiled, so use dyes that can be dry-cleaned. Cottons can be boiled so use dyes that can withstand high temperatures.

1 Break away as much of the hardened wax as you can. Do not scrub at the cloth as this may damage the surface.

2 Place the batik between two pieces of newsprint, brown or lining paper and iron until the wax is absorbed into the paper. Remember to remove the paper while the wax is still molten. Repeat the process with clean pieces of paper until wax is no longer absorbed. Check the setting method of a dye before washing.

3 To use the boiling method you must be sure to use a dye that does not need ironing in order to be fixed (reactive dyes are the most suitable). Break off as much wax as possible (step 1), and then place the cloth in boiling water for about ten minutes, stirring continuously.

4 After boiling, place the cloth in cold water. The wax will solidify in the water and can be strained or lightly brushed away from the surface of the cloth. Do not pour any wax down the drain. Allow the water to cool, then remove wax by straining. Repeat steps 3 and 4, if necessary, until all the wax is removed.

## Cracking

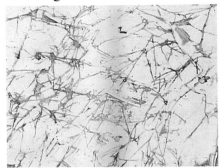

To achieve a crackled effect, the cotton fabric was coated in a layer of wax. It was crumpled, resulting in the surface of the wax cracking. The cloth can be dyed using the direct method, though for best results it should be dyed in a dye bath and use a brittle crackle wax.

## Using a Canting

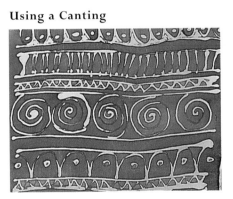

The canting allows delicate designs to be drawn on to the cloth with wax. When using a canting, wipe the exterior to remove any molten wax. Wax on the base of the canting may smudge on to the cloth and ruin the design. Keep your movement light when working with the canting and do not press down too hard on to the fabric as this may block the flow of wax.

## Using a Decorating Brush

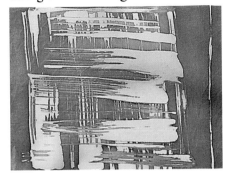

This cross-hatching effect was made using a medium-sized decorating brush. Lightly draw the waxed brush across the undyed cloth horizontally and then vertically. Do not press down hard with the brush as this will produce solid blocks of wax. Different sizes of brush can be used.

## Ragging

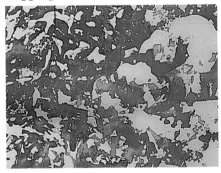

Scrunch up a piece of lightweight fabric or kitchen paper (paper towel), dip it in the molten wax and then press it firmly on to the surface of the undyed cloth. If you find that the wax is setting before it is transferred to the cloth you may wish to change the rag to one with a tighter weave (pongee silk works well) as these hold the heat better.

# PAPIER-MÂCHÉ BOWL

THIS BOWL WAS MADE WITH A TISSUE PAPER PAPIER-MÂCHÉ AND DECORATED WITH GOLD INK. THE WAX WILL NOT SINK INTO THE PAPIER-MÂCHÉ IN THE SAME WAY AS IT WOULD WITH FABRIC, BUT IT SHOULD STICK FIRMLY TO THE BOWL IF IT BRUSHES AWAY EASILY, IT IS NOT HOT ENOUGH AND SHOULD BE RE-APPLIED.

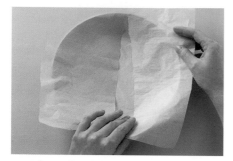

**1** Select a bowl that is a suitable size and shape. Line the bowl with dry tissue paper. This will help when the time comes to remove the finished bowl from the mould.

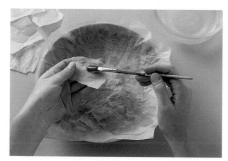

**2** Make the bowl by applying wallpaper paste to squares of tissue paper and placing layers of glued paper inside the mould. Each layer should be placed in the opposite direction to the last. Place two layers of pink tissue as the central two layers with four layers of pale blue on either side. The dye from the pink paper will seep through the blue paper to leave a mottled pattern on the surface of the bowl.

**3** Make 10 layers in all for the bowl. Leave it to dry thoroughly. Remove the bowl from the mould and trim the sides to a nice neat edge. Melt the wax. Using a brush, apply rings of wax inside the bowl, starting from the bottom and working out towards the rim.

**4** Using gold ink, paint the inside of the bowl, so that you get alternate strips of gold and wax. Leave the bowl to dry thoroughly.

**5** Heat the inside of the bowl with a hairdryer until the wax is molten. Wipe the molten wax around the inside of the bowl with a rag, absorbing any excess wax.

**6** Paint the outside (bottom) of the bowl with wax. It is not necessary to paint wax right up to the rim. The sides can be left. Again, heat the wax with a hairdryer until it is molten. Allow the wax to run down the sides of the bowl towards the rim. Rub the wax into the surface of the bowl with a rag. Remove any excess with a rag. Paint the bowl with clear lacquer to give it extra protection.

## MATERIALS AND EQUIPMENT YOU WILL NEED
BOWL • TISSUE PAPER • WALLPAPER PASTE • PAPER SCISSORS • MEDIUM BRUSH • GENERAL-PURPOSE WAX • WAX POT OR DOUBLE BOILER •
GOLD INK • ARTIST'S BRUSH (FOR INK) • HAIRDRYER • RAGS • CLEAR LACQUER (USED FOR NON-POROUS SURFACES SUCH AS BRASS) • BRUSH

# SILK SQUARE SCARF

THE SQUARE SILK SCARF CAN BE BOUGHT WITH THE EDGES READY-ROLLED. WE HAVE USED CRÊPE DE CHINE BUT ANY LIGHTWEIGHT SILK CAN BE USED.

HEAT-FIXED SILK PAINTS NEED TO BE USED TO ALLOW SEVERAL LAYERS OF DYE TO BE PAINTED ON TOP OF EACH OTHER.

**1** Enlarge the design from the template on to tracing paper. The template is one-quarter of the actual size of the design. The whole scarf is 30 x 30 in (76 x 76 cm). Pin the silk scarf to a frame. Place the design face down on to the corner of the scarf, 7 cm (3 in) from both sides, on the front of the scarf. Using a soft pencil, trace the design on to the back of the silk. To make the whole design, reverse the template so that the wider corner is always at the outer edge. Repeat the design in the remaining sections so that the wide border is around the edge of the scarf.

**2** Heat the wax and apply it in spirals on the fabric using a canting. Keep your movements nice and light and make sure that the exterior of the canting is free of molten wax as this may smudge on to your work.

**3** Using a sponge brush, paint the light blue dye over the whole scarf. Allow the dye to bleed from the brush rather than overloading the fabric with dye. Overloading can cause uneven colour. Leave to dry. ▶

## MATERIALS AND EQUIPMENT YOU WILL NEED

TRACING PAPER • PENCIL • RULER • SILK PINS • CRÊPE DE CHINE SILK, 90 CM (36 IN) SQUARE • WOODEN FRAME, 90 CM (36 IN) SQUARE •
GENERAL-PURPOSE WAX • WAX POT OR DOUBLE BOILER • CANTING (MEDIUM SPOUT) • SPONGE BRUSH •
IRON-FIX DYES: LIGHT BLUE, ROYAL BLUE, LILAC, PURPLE, DARK BLUE • BOWLS • BRUSH (FOR WAX), 4 CM (1½ IN) WIDE •
KITCHEN PAPER (PAPER TOWEL) • IRON • NEWSPRINT, BROWN OR LINING PAPER • NEEDLE AND THREAD

4 Using a brush, apply the wax in a grid shape.

6 Use the same brush to apply the wax and cover the coloured areas with a wax brushstroke.

7 Paint dark blue dye over the whole scarf. Blot any excess dye with kitchen paper towels. Leave the fabric to dry.

5 Paint the royal blue, lilac and purple dye in the squares. Leave to dry.

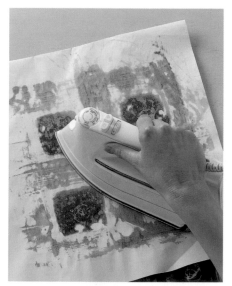

8 Iron the scarf between sheets of newsprint, brown or lining paper. The heat will set the dye. Keep changing the paper until no more wax appears. Have the scarf dry-cleaned to remove the excess wax. Hem the scarf by rolling the edges.

# ABSTRACT PICTURE

JOAN MIRÓ IS THE INSPIRATION FOR THIS COLOURFUL ABSTRACT DESIGN. BLACK FABRIC CAN BE USED WHEN BLACK IS A PROMINENT COLOUR. THE BLACK FAB-RIC MUST BE TESTED TO CHECK WHETHER IT CAN BE BLEACHED. AT THE END OF THE PROCESS, A RESIDUE OF WAX IS LEFT IN THE FABRIC TO KEEP IT SLIGHTLY STIFF.

1 Enlarge and trace the template on to tracing paper using a black pen. This should be the size of the finished picture. Pin the black fabric to the frame. Secure the paper design to the back of the fabric using masking tape. Hold the frame up to a light source and lightly trace the design on the front of the fabric, using a piece of chalk.

2 Heat the wax and apply it with a brush to the areas that will remain black. Check that the wax has penetrated through to the back of the fabric. If necessary, wax the same area from the back.

3 Wearing rubber gloves and working in a well-ventilated area, remove the fabric from the frame and place it in a bowl of thin bleach. Use just enough bleach to cover the fabric. Leave the fabric in the bleach until it has turned cream. Agitate the fabric to allow even bleaching.

4 Rinse the fabric in water, then rinse in water with a splash of vinegar to neutralize the bleach. Rinse in water again. Pin the fabric back on the frame and leave it to dry. ▶

## MATERIALS AND EQUIPMENT YOU WILL NEED

TRACING PAPER • BLACK PEN • RULER • DRAWING PINS • THIN BLACK COTTON (BLEACHABLE), 65 x 45 CM (26 x 18 IN) • FRAME, 65 x 45 CM (26 x 18 IN) • MASKING TAPE • CHALK • GENERAL-PURPOSE WAX • WAX POT OR DOUBLE BOILER • MEDIUM BRUSH • RUBBER GLOVES • BOWL • THIN BLEACH • VINEGAR • DYES: RED, YELLOW, ORANGE, BLUE AND GREEN • SMALL BOWLS FOR DYES • DYE BRUSH • IRON • NEWSPRINT, BROWN OR LINING PAPER • SEWING MACHINE • BLACK THREAD • 2 PIECES OF DOWELLING, 50 CM (20 IN) LONG • FISHING WIRE OR STRING

**5** Check that the waxed lines are solid. Re-wax any black lines that are cracked. Paint the different coloured dyes in the non-waxed areas, according to the manufacturer's instructions. Leave to dry.

**6** Apply wax to the coloured areas so that all the fabric is covered in wax. This is to avoid a wax shadow on the final picture. Remove the fabric from the frame. Iron the cloth between sheets of newsprint, brown or lining paper. Continue ironing, replacing the sheets of paper until no more wax appears through the paper. The cloth will remain slightly stiff.

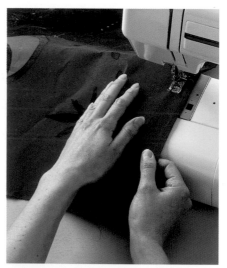

**7** Hem both sides of the picture. Sew a 2 cm (¾ in) hem at the top and the bottom. Insert a piece of 1 cm (½ in) dowelling at both ends. Attach a piece of fishing wire or string to both ends of the top piece of dowelling to allow for hanging.

# PASTEL BLIND

THIS BLIND WAS MADE FROM MOSTLY PASTEL PAPERS, ALTHOUGH WATER-COLOUR PAPERS CAN BE USED. HANDMADE JAPANESE PAPERS ARE NICE FOR TEXTURE THOUGH THEY ARE EXPENSIVE. THE WOODEN BARS WITH THE SPRING MOTION USED FOR ROLLER BLINDS CAN BE BOUGHT IN VARIOUS SIZES.

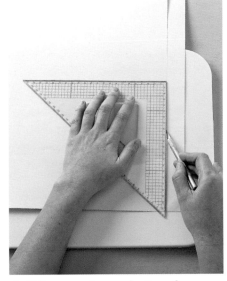

1 Collect together a selection of paper in soft, muted colours. Trim the papers down to squares and rectangles about 29 cm (11½ in) wide. These blocks of papers will be joined together in a patch-work to make up the blind.

2 Enlarge and trace the flower shapes at the back of the book on to the papers. Place some of the flowers at angles so that they look scattered, not neatly arranged.

3 Wax in the flower outlines with a canting. The wax should stick firmly to the paper. If it brushes off easily, the wax is not hot enough.

4 Using a fine artist's brush and some inks, paint in details on the flower shapes, such as the leaves and petals. ▶

MATERIALS AND EQUIPMENT YOU WILL NEED

SELECTION OF PAPERS (PASTEL, WATERCOLOUR AND HAND-MADE JAPANESE) • CRAFT KNIFE • TRACING PAPER • PENCIL • RULER •
GENERAL-PURPOSE WAX • WAX POT OR DOUBLE BOILER • CANTING • FINE ARTIST'S BRUSHES (FOR INK) • INKS • SPONGE BRUSH • HAIRDRYER •
RAG • DOUBLE-SIDED TAPE • EMBROIDERY THREAD (FLOSS) AND NEEDLE • ROLLER BLIND KIT • SET (T) SQUARE OR RULER • LARGE BEAD

5 Using a sponge brush and inks paint in the background to the flower design. Keep the brushstrokes loose so that you develop a painterly textured effect.

6 When the inks have dried, heat the applied wax until molten with a hairdryer. Rub the molten wax into the paper with a rag, spreading it as much as possible. By rubbing the wax into the blind you not only add texture but also make the blind more durable and water-resistant.

7 Stick two pieces of paper batik together with double-sided tape. It is best not to place the tape right next to the edge of the paper but to have a 5 mm (¼ in) gap. This will give you room to sew the two pieces of paper together.

8 With some embroidery thread (floss) sew up the join (seam) between the papers. It is best not to sew through the double-sided tape as this can be quite stiff and may tear the papers. Trim each of these sections down so that they are the correct width for your blind. Continue joining the paper batiks together in this way until you have enough width sections to make up the length of the blind.

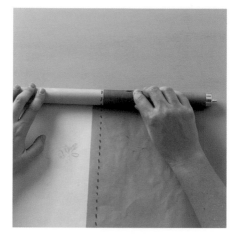

9 Join all the width sections of paper together to make up the length of the blind, sticking and sewing in the same way as before. Stick the top of the patch-work paper to the top baton of the roller blind kit (refer to the manufacturer's instructions).

10 Stick the bottom baton to the paper using double-sided tape. The top and bottom baton can be over-stitched for added security by wrapping embroidery thread through the paper and round each button. To make the blind easier to pull up and down, tie a bead around the bottom baton of the blind using embroidery thread.

# TABLE MATS

THESE TABLE MATS WERE DYED USING THE DIRECT DYEING METHOD WITH IRON-FIX DYES. THEY WERE PADDED TO MAKE THEM BETTER AT ABSORBING HEAT AND PROTECTING TABLETOPS. USE A DURABLE FABRIC, SUCH AS COTTON, AND DYES THAT ARE FAST IN QUITE HOT WASHING TEMPERATURES.

**1** Pin some fine white cotton on to a frame. Ensure that the frame is big enough for the mat, about 34 cm x 23 cm (13½ x 9 in), with at least 2 cm (¾ in) wastage. Enlarge the template until it is the size required for your mat.

**2** Turn the frame upside down on to the design and trace using a water-soluble dressmaker's pen. The design should show through on the face of the cloth. If the design is not visible through the cotton, trace the design on to the surface of the cloth using tracing paper.

**3** Heat the wax to a steady 120°C (248°F) and, using a canting, wax the outline of the cup shapes. You could also wax a line around the edge of the cloth to keep your work neat. Check the back of the cloth to make sure that the wax has penetrated sufficiently.

**4** Fill in the background to the cups with sky blue dye using a brush. Fill in the cup shapes with yellow dye. Do not over-load the cloth with dye, as it might bleed under the wax barrier. When applying dye, allow it to bleed out from the brush.

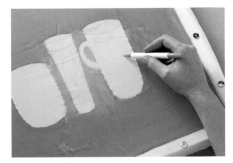

**5** Draw the pattern on the cup shapes using a water-soluble dressmaker's pen. Wax the details in using a canting. Check the back for breaks in the wax outline and if necessary re-apply molten wax to the back.

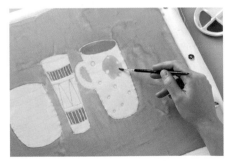

**6** Paint in more colours to the cup details. When you overpaint the cup shapes, it is important to consider how one colour dye will affect another. For example, yellow over-painted with blue will make green. ▶

---

MATERIALS AND EQUIPMENT YOU WILL NEED

LIGHTWEIGHT WHITE COTTON • FRAME • SILK PINS • WATER-SOLUBLE DRESSMAKER'S PEN • TRACING PAPER (OPTIONAL) • GENERAL-PURPOSE WAX • WAX POT OR DOUBLE BOILER • CANTING • FABRIC DYES • MEDIUM BRUSH • IRON • NEWSPRINT, BROWN OR LINING PAPER • SCISSORS • MEDIUM WADDING (BATTING) • BACKING CLOTH • SEWING MACHINE AND THREAD • BIAS BINDING • PINS • EMBROIDERY THREAD (FLOSS) • NEEDLE

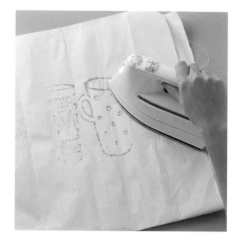

**7** Remove the batik from the frame and iron out as much wax as possible using newsprint, brown or lining paper. Because the mats are made from cotton, grease marks and wax residue can be removed using the boiling process (see Finishing). Otherwise, have the table mat dry-cleaned when it is completed.

**9** Open up a piece of bias binding long enough to run down the side of the mat and, with the reverse side of the binding facing out, line up the right edge with the reverse right edge of the mat. Pin in place. Sew down the edge of the mat following the crease on the bias binding as a guide. Do this on both sides of the mat.

**11** Repeat steps 9 and 10 with the top and the bottom of the mat. Rather than cutting the ends square, fold these in before topstitching in order to give nice neat corners.

**8** Trim down the batik to table mat size (don't include any seam allowances). Cut a piece of medium thickness wadding (batting) and a piece of backing cloth to the same size. Tack (baste) the three pieces together using a sewing machine.

**10** Fold the bias binding on to the right side of the mat and topstitch, keeping as close to the edge of the binding as you can. Trim the top and bottom of the bound edge so that they are square with the top and bottom of the mat.

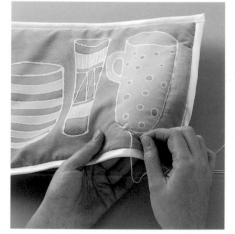

**12** Using embroidery thread (floss), sew extra details on to the cup design. Sewing straight through the mat will result in a quilted effect.

# SHAWL

THIS SCARF HAS ONLY BEEN DECORATED AT BOTH ENDS, ALTHOUGH THE PATTERN COULD BE CONTINUED DOWN THE WHOLE LENGTH. A CANTING WAS USED TO DRAW THE WAX PATTERNS ON TO A FINE PONGEE SILK, AND IRON-FIX SILK PAINTS WERE USED TO ADD COLOUR. WHEN CHOOSING THE SIZE OF THE SCARF, REMEMBER TO ADD 5 CM (2 IN) ALL AROUND THE EDGES TO GIVE YOURSELF ENOUGH ROOM TO TRIM AWAY EDGES AND FINISH THE SCARF. AS WE HAVE ONLY DECORATED A BORDER WE USED A SMALL PAINTING FRAME, ALTHOUGH IF YOU WANT TO DECORATE THE WHOLE SCARF YOU MAY NEED TO MAKE YOUR OWN FRAME.

1 Enlarge the template design using a photocopier so that it is the correct length for your decorated border. The design will fit side to side. Transfer the design to tracing paper using a black pen and set (T) square.

2 Pin one end of the silk to a frame. Choose a frame that is slightly deeper than the height of the border design; remember to allow for wastage all round.

3 Turn the frame upside down on to the design and trace off all horizontal lines using a soft pencil or water-soluble dressmaker's pen.

4 Heat the wax to a steady 120°C (248°F) and wax in all horizontal stripes using a canting. Remember to close in the ends of each stripe to contain the dye and prevent bleeding. The cloth should appear semi-transparent when waxed. If areas of the cloth remain opaque, re-apply the molten wax to the back in these areas. ▶

## MATERIALS AND EQUIPMENT YOU WILL NEED

TRACING PAPER • PEN • SET (T) SQUARE • LIGHTWEIGHT HABOTAI SILK • PAINTING FRAME • SILK PINS • SOFT PENCIL OR WATER-SOLUBLE DRESS-MAKER'S PEN • GENERAL-PURPOSE WAX • WAX POT OR DOUBLE BOILER • CANTING • IRON-FIX SILK PAINTS • PAINTBRUSH • HAIRDRYER • IRON • NEWSPRINT, BROWN OR LINING PAPER • SCISSORS • NEEDLE AND THREAD

5 Fill in the stripes with pale colours, such as smoky blue, terracotta or pale pink. If you are diluting dyes, always check the manufacturer's guidelines for maximum dye and dilutent ratios.

7 Paint over the stripes and details with darker dyes such as purple, blue, deep red and brown. Repeat steps 1 to 7 with the other end of the scarf.

9 Trim off the wastage. If possible, tear the cloth to ensure a straight edge.

6 When the silk is dry, fix the dyes with the heat from a hairdryer; be careful when doing this not to melt the wax. Replace the frame upside down on to the design and trace off the detail and the patterning. Wax in these details with a canting, working slowly and carefully.

8 If possible, remove some hardened wax with your fingers from the cloth. Then iron the batik between two pieces of newsprint, brown or lining paper to remove the majority of the wax. Repeat the process until the paper is no longer absorbing the wax. The fabric will still be quite stiff at this stage.

10 Finally, roll the edges of the silk and sew them into place. It is best to have the finished scarf dry-cleaned in order to restore the drape and sheen of the silk.

# PICTURE FRAME

IT IS IMPORTANT WHEN APPLYING WAX OR COLOUR TO A WOODEN SURFACE THAT YOU USE UNTREATED OR "NUDE" WOOD WITH A SMOOTH SURFACE. WOOD THAT HAS BEEN VARNISHED OR WAXED WILL NOT ABSORB COLOUR; NEITHER WILL IT ALLOW WAX TO ADHERE TO IT SUFFICIENTLY. REMEMBER TO REMOVE ALL THE DUST FROM THE WOOD GRAIN WITH A RAG OR DRY BRUSH BEFORE STARTING AS, AGAIN, THIS WILL AFFECT THE APPLICATION OF WOOD STAIN OR WAX.

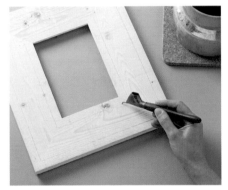

1 Draw around the frame on to a piece of tracing paper and work out the design to scale or enlarge the template. Allow for a narrow border on the inside and outside edge.

3 Heat the wax. Wax in the ruled lines with a canting. Make sure there are no breaks in the line; the wax should stick firmly to the surface of the wood. If it brushes away easily, it is not hot enough.

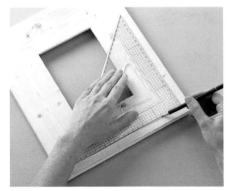

5 Run masking tape around the edge of the borders to protect the central frame area.

2 Using a ruler, draw the borders on all the edges of the frame. These borders will be textured with a stipple brush.

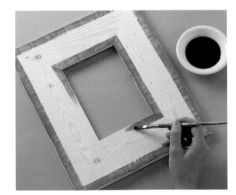

4 Paint the borders with a rust-coloured wood stain, such as willow. Leave the frame to dry thoroughly.

6 Use a stubby stencil brush to dab wax on to the frame borders. Do not apply too much wax, as some wood must be left free of wax so that more colours can be applied. ▶

## MATERIALS AND EQUIPMENT YOU WILL NEED

UNTREATED WOODEN FREE-STANDING FRAME • PENCIL (HB) • TRACING PAPER • RULER • GENERAL-PURPOSE WAX •
WAX POT OR DOUBLE BOILER • CANTING • MEDIUM SOFT BRUSHES (FOR WOOD STAIN) • WOOD STAIN: WILLOW, MAHOGANY AND OLIVE GREEN •
MASKING TAPE • STENCIL BRUSH (SHORT HAIRED) • ERASER (OPTIONAL) • HAIRDRYER • RAGS

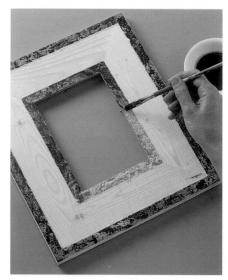

7 Remove the masking tape. Over-paint the waxed borders with a mahogany wood stain and leave to dry completely.

9 Wax in the leaf design with a canting, blocking in the leaves with wax. Once again, make sure that the wax sticks firmly to the surface of the wood.

10 Over-paint the leaf design and central area of the frame with an olive-green wood stain.

8 Place the design from step 1 on top of the frame and trace the leaf pattern. The pencil marks on the wood should be as light as possible. If necessary, use an eraser to remove some of the pencil.

11 When the frame is dry, heat the wax with a hairdryer until the wax becomes molten. Rub the molten wax into the surface of the wood with a rag. Try to spread the wax as much as possible across the surface of the frame, as this will help to bring out the colour of the wood stains.

# CUSHION COVER

THIS BRIGHTLY COLOURED CUSHION COVER WAS MADE USING A TWO-TONE ORANGE AND PINK DOUPION SILK AS THE BASE COLOUR. THE CUSHION PAD IS SIMPLY INSERTED INTO THE COVER THROUGH AN OPENING. CHOOSE A FABRIC AND COLOUR SCHEME TO MATCH YOUR INTERIOR DECOR.

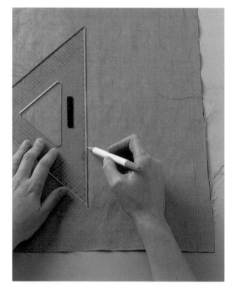

1 On a piece of silk, mark a 42 cm (17 in) square with a pencil (this is for a 40 cm (16 in) cushion pad, allowing for a 1 cm (½ in) seam allowance). Mark a grid with a water-soluble dressmaker's pen in the centre. The grid should be three squares across and three squares down, each square measuring 10 cm (4 in).

2 Pin the silk on to a frame, making sure it is stretched nice and tight. It should be springy to the touch.

3 Heat the wax. Wax in the grid using a canting. It is important that there are no breaks in the outline, so check the back for areas of fabric that remain opaque once the wax has been applied. Fill in any breaks with wax on the back.

## MATERIALS AND EQUIPMENT YOU WILL NEED

DOUPION SILK (TWO-TONE PINK AND ORANGE) • PENCIL • RULER • SET (T) SQUARE • WATER-SOLUBLE DRESSMAKER'S PEN • SILK PINS • FRAME • GENERAL-PURPOSE WAX • WAX POT OR DOUBLE BOILER • CANTING • IRON-FIX SILK PAINTS – BLUE, RED, OLIVE GREEN, PURPLE AND BROWN • BRUSHES (FOR DYE) • IRON • NEWSPRINT, BROWN OR LINING PAPER • SCISSORS • SEWING MACHINE AND THREAD • PINS • CUSHION PAD

4 Fill in the grid with diluted blue, red, olive green and brown silk paints. Allow the dye to blend out from the brush to the wax outline rather than overloading the fabric with dye as this may cause the colour to bleed underneath the wax.

5 Once the dye is dry, draw in the remainder of the design, squares within squares. Do not use a ruler for this. It will add to the effect if the squares are slightly irregular.

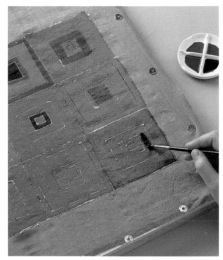

6 Wax in the remainder of the design. Again, check the back for breaks in the wax outline. Fill in the remaining colours using deep reds, purples, olive green and brown. Use a different brush for each colour or make sure you dry the brush after each rinsing. If wet brushes are used, the dyes will become diluted.

7 Remove the silk from the frame and iron out all the wax. To remove any final grease marks, have the finished cover dry-cleaned.

8 Trim the fabric down to the marked 42 cm (17 in) square, allowing for a 2.5 cm (1 in) seam. Cut two rectangles of silk measuring 42 x 28 cm (17 x 11 in) and sew a double turnover (turn over by 1 cm (½ in), iron and turn again). These two hemmed edges of cloth will fall in the centre back of the cushion cover.

9 Place the square of silk with the batik design face up on the work surface. Place the silk rectangles on top, face down, with the hemmed edges in the centre. Pin or baste the pieces together around the edge. ▶

**10** Machine stitch all the way round the cushion cover, leaving a 1 cm (½ in) seam allowance. Sew a line of zigzag stitches between the sewn seam and the raw edge. This will prevent fraying.

**11** Finally, turn the cover the right side out. Dry-clean the cover if necessary and insert a cushion pad.

# COTTON SARONG

THE FABRIC CAN BE WAXED ON A PLASTIC SURFACE AND THE MATERIAL MOVED ALONG AFTER EACH SECTION HAS BEEN COMPLETED. THE TRADITIONAL CRACKLE EFFECT HAPPENS NATURALLY WHEN THE FABRIC IS DYED. USING THE CRACKLE IN A BORDER NEXT TO A PLAIN COLOUR MAKES AN EFFECTIVE CONTRAST.

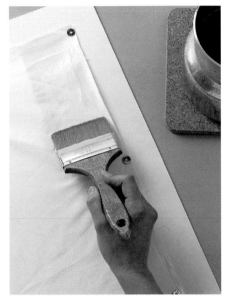

**1** Trace the templates on to a piece of tracing paper. Cut them out secure them on to the sponge. Draw around the template. With a craft knife or scalpel, cut out the sponge shapes.

**2** Pin or stick one end of the cotton on to a plastic board. Heat the wax. Apply the wax with a large brush around the edge of the sarong.

**3** Use the circle sponge and apply the wax, leaving approximately 8 cm (3¼ in) between each circle. Repeat the pattern around the edge of the border. ▶

### MATERIALS AND EQUIPMENT YOU WILL NEED

TRACING PAPER • PENCIL • SCISSORS • PINS OR MASKING TAPE • SPONGE • CRAFT KNIFE • 1.5 M (60 IN) THIN COTTON, 90 CM (36 IN) WIDE • PLASTIC BOARD OR SURFACE • GENERAL-PURPOSE WAX • WAX POT OR DOUBLE BOILER • LARGE BRUSH, 8 CM (3¼ IN) WIDE • LARGE BOWL • LATEX GLOVES • BUCKET OR TRAY • DYES: YELLOW AND DARK GREEN • IRON • NEWSPRINT, BROWN OR LINING PAPER • NEEDLE AND THREAD OR SEWING MACHINE

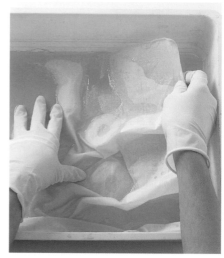

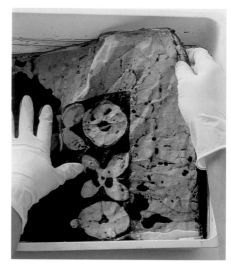

4 Place the fabric in a large bowl of water to wet it thoroughly. Then put the wet fabric in a bucket or tray of yellow dye according to the manufacturer's instructions. Hang up the fabric to dry.

6 Place the fabric in a large bowl of water, then put the wet fabric in a bucket or tray of dark-green dye, according to the manufacturer's instructions. Hang up the fabric to dry.

7 Iron the fabric between sheets of newsprint, brown or lining paper, until no more wax appears through the paper. Have the fabric dry-cleaned to remove the excess wax.

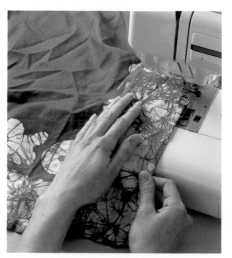

5 Pin or stick the fabric back on to the plastic board. Using the same brush, re-wax the border to keep the yellow crackle effect. Also, wax over the circles again using the same sponge stencil. Take the cross stencil and apply the wax between the circles.

8 Turn over the raw edges, about 1 cm (½ in) and sew to neaten them. There is no need to neaten the selvedge.

# SILK VELVET MUFFLER

THE BATIK EFFECT ON SILK VELVET GIVES A DISTINCTIVE MOTTLED LOOK TO THE FABRIC. THE VELVET NEEDS TO BE WAXED ON A PLASTIC SURFACE, AND A SPONGE IS USED TO HELP THE WAX PENETRATE THROUGH THE PILE. AT LEAST TWO LAYERS OF WAX MUST BE APPLIED ON THE SAME AREA TO PROTECT THE VELVET THOROUGHLY. CONSEQUENTLY, IT TAKES A LONG TIME TO IRON THE WAX OFF. IF REACTIVE DYES ARE USED, ADD A SPLASH OF VINEGAR FOR EACH LITRE OF DYE.

1 Draw a diamond shape on to a piece of tracing paper. Cut it out and draw around it on to the sponge. Cut out the diamond shape on the sponge with a craft knife or scalpel.

2 Pin or stick one end of the velvet muffler on to a board or plastic surface. Apply the wax in three rows using the diamond-shaped sponge stencil, following the design. Apply the single wax diamonds randomly along the length of the scarf. Re-pin the scarf at the opposite end and then repeat the design. Repeat the same waxing process again to completely protect the white velvet. Remove the fabric from the board.

3 Place the fabric in a bowl of water. Then put the wet fabric in a large tray of gold dye, agitate and remove after approximately three minutes. Blot between sheets of newsprint to remove excess dye, then hang up to dry. ▶

## MATERIALS AND EQUIPMENT YOU WILL NEED

TRACING PAPER • PENCIL • SCISSORS • SPONGE • CRAFT KNIFE • SILK / VISCOSE VELVET, 130 x 27 CM (52 x 10½ IN) • SILK PINS OR TAPE • PLASTIC BOARD • GENERAL-PURPOSE WAX • WAX POT OR DOUBLE BOILER • BOWL • TRAY • DYE: GOLD AND DARK BROWN • NEWSPRINT, BROWN OR LINING PAPER • IRON • KNIFE • SEWING MACHINE AND THREAD • NEEDLE

4 Pin the fabric to the plastic board. Wax the gold areas using the sponge stencil, following the design. Repeat the waxing to protect the gold velvet. Roughly wax over the white diamonds again, to keep the gold crackle effect. Remove the fabric from the board.

6 Iron the velvet between sheets of newsprint, brown or lining paper with the pile side down. When the wax is partially melted, turn the velvet over and scrape the softened, excess wax off the pile with a knife. Turn the velvet over again and keep ironing until most of the wax has been absorbed by the paper. Even after ironing the velvet will remain very stiff. Have the velvet dry-cleaned to remove the excess wax.

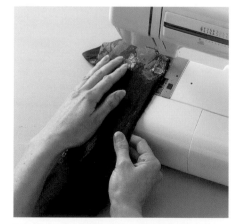

5 Place the fabric in a bowl of water, then put the wet fabric in dark brown dye. Agitate for approximately three minutes. Blot between sheets of newsprint and hang up the fabric to dry.

7 Sew the fabric together lengthwise with right sides facing. Leave an 8 cm (3¼ in) gap halfway down the side and turn the scarf the right way round. Hand sew the gap. Steam iron the seams flat.

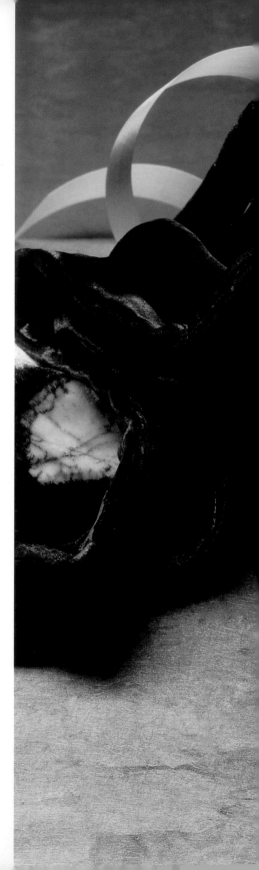

# LEATHER BOOKMARK

THIS BOOKMARK IS EASY TO MAKE FROM A SMALL SCRAP OF NATURAL LEATHER. IT IS DECORATED WITH THREE COLOURS OF LEATHER DYE USING GUM INSTEAD OF WAX AS THE RESIST TO ACHIEVE THE BATIK EFFECT. THE LEATHER MUST BE DAMPENED SLIGHTLY BEFORE CUTTING AND MARKING THE DESIGN.

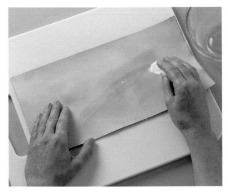

1 Dampen the leather with a piece of cotton wool ball dipped in water.

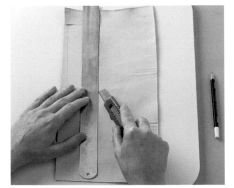

2 Cut out the piece for the bookmark from the leather with a craft knife. Work on a cutting mat to protect the underlying surface.

3 Enlarge and trace the template or draw your own design on white paper. Transfer the design from the paper on to the leather.

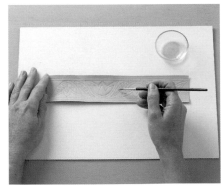

4 Allow the leather to dry completely before using the gum. Apply the gum with a brush on the leather to those areas you want to remain white (or natural leather colour).

5 Make a pad from a piece of soft cloth and cotton wool ball and dip it into the yellow dye. Wear latex gloves to protect your hands. Press the pad on to a scrap of leather to remove any excess dye and then, beginning in one corner, move the pad from left to right over the surface of the leather. Once the whole area has been coated, leave it to dry naturally.

▶

MATERIALS AND EQUIPMENT YOU WILL NEED

TRACING PAPER • PENCIL • COTTON WOOL (BALLS) • LEATHER • CRAFT KNIFE • CUTTING MAT • GUM • BRUSH • SPONGE DAUBER • SOFT CLOTH • LEATHER DYE: YELLOW, RED AND BLACK • LATEX GLOVES • LEATHER LACQUER SPRAY • PINKING SHEARS • PAPER OR FABRIC (OPTIONAL)

6 When dry, cover the yellow part of the design with gum. Apply red dye on the leather with a cotton wool ball or pad. When completely dry, block out those areas that are to remain red.

8 You are now ready to dye the bookmark with last colour black. Use a sponge dauber to achieve good coverage.

10 Allow the leather to dry completely and spray with lacquer to protect it. Finish the bookmark by trimming the edges with pinking shears for a decorative effect. You can then cover the back with paper or fabric to finish.

7 Before using the black dye, crumple the leather well to achieve a good crackled effect.

9 With a large piece of cotton wool (ball), remove the gum by washing with plenty of cold water.

# STORAGE BOX

THIS STORAGE BOX WAS DYED USING WOOD STAIN AND DECORATED WITH A PRETTY FLORAL DESIGN. USE IT TO STORE JEWELLERY OR GIVE IT TO A FRIEND FOR A SPECIAL BIRTHDAY GIFT. WHEN APPLYING WAX OR WOODSTAIN IT IS IMPORTANT TO USE "NUDE" OR UNTREATED WOOD.

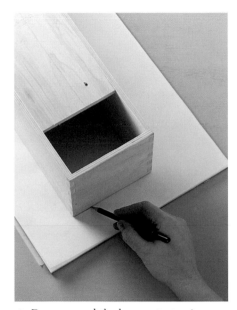

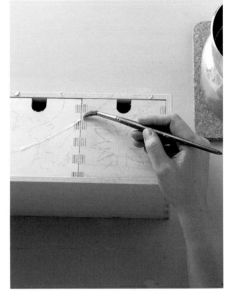

1 Draw around the box on to tracing paper. Work out the design, and draw this to size, on the tracing paper. Allow some of the stems and tendrils to go from the face of the box on to the topside.

2 Trace the design on to the wood. Keep the pencil marks on the wood very faint. Use a plastic eraser to remove some of the markings if necessary.

3 Heat the wax. Use a brush to apply molten wax to the flower stems on your design. The wax should stick firmly to the surface of the wood; if it brushes away easily the wax is not hot enough and should be re-applied. ▶

## MATERIALS AND EQUIPMENT YOU WILL NEED

UNTREATED WOODEN STORAGE BOX • TRACING PAPER • PENCIL • PLASTIC ERASER (OPTIONAL) • FINE ARTIST'S BRUSH (FOR WAX) • GENERAL-PURPOSE WAX • WAX POT OR DOUBLE BOILER • CANTING • WOOD STAIN: WILLOW, DARK MAHOGANY • FINE AND MEDIUM BRUSHES (FOR STAIN) • HAIRDRYER • RAG

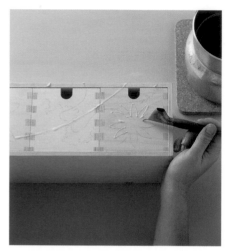

4 Using a canting, draw the outline of the leaves and the flower shapes. As in step 3, make sure the wax is firmly stuck to the surface of the wood. It is important that there are no breaks in these outlines, as this will allow one colour to bleed into the next.

6 Fill in the leaves with a rusty brown (willow) wood stain. Allow the stain to bleed from the brush to the wax outline rather than overloading the edges with colour. This will help to prevent the dyes from bleeding under the wax.

8 Paint the entire box with a dark mahogany wood stain. Again, be careful not to overload the stain around the waxed outlines to avoid the stain bleeding under the wax.

5 Using the canting, make small spots in the flower's centre. You could alternatively add texture to this area by cutting a stencil and ragging or splashing wax (see Basic Techniques).

7 Fill in the entire flower shape with the rusty brown wood stain. Make sure to over-paint the textured area at the centre of the flower so that the stain is able to penetrate. Allow to dry.

9 When the wood stain is thoroughly dry, heat the surface of the wood with a hairdryer until the wax is molten. Rub the molten wax firmly on to the surface of the wood with a rag. Try to spread the wax as much as possible across the surface of the wood, as this will help to bring out the colour of the wood stains.

# GEOMETRIC-STYLED NAPKIN

WHEN MAKING A NAPKIN OR OTHER ITEM THAT NEEDS REPEATED WASHING, USE A DYE THAT STAYS FAST IN MEDIUM-WASHING TEMPERATURES. IN THIS PROJECT, WE DECORATED A READY-MADE WHITE COTTON NAPKIN, WHICH WAS WASHED AT THE MANUFACTURER'S MAXIMUM SUGGESTED HEAT SETTING TO REMOVE ANY FINISHING LEFT IN THE CLOTH. IF YOU WISH TO MAKE YOUR OWN NAPKIN, USE A DURABLE LIGHTWEIGHT NATURAL FIBRE SUCH AS COTTON OR LINEN.

1 Draw a 10 cm (4 in) cross in the centre of the napkin with a pencil. Pin the napkin to a frame, making sure it is stretched nice and taut.

2 Turn the frame upside down on to your design, lining up the central cross on the fabric with the central cross of the design. Trace your design on to the cloth using a pencil or a water-soluble dressmaker's pen that will show through the fabric. If the design is not visible through the fabric, use tracing paper to transfer the design.

3 Heat the wax to 120°C (248°F). Draw in the main square with wax using a canting. It is imperative that there are no breaks in this wax outline. The cloth should appear semi-transparent when waxed. Check the back of the cloth for areas of the cloth that remain opaque; re-apply the molten wax to the back in these areas. ▶

## MATERIALS AND EQUIPMENT YOU WILL NEED

HB PENCIL • RULER • WHITE COTTON NAPKIN • SILK PINS • SQUARE FRAME • WATER-SOLUBLE DRESSMAKER'S PEN • TRACING PAPER •
GENERAL-PURPOSE WAX • WAX POT OR DOUBLE BOILER • CANTING • FABRIC DYE: SKY BLUE, LILAC AND COBALT BLUE •
MEDIUM ARTISTS SPONGES (FOR DYE) • IRON • NEWSPRINT, BROWN OR LINING PAPER

4 Fill in the central square with sky blue dye. Do not overload the cloth with dye, or the blue dye may bleed into the white border. Allow the dye to bleed from the brush, especially when working near the wax outline.

6 Paint the central square with a dye (lilac). Once again, do not overload the cloth with dye.

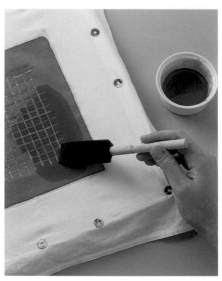

8 Using a sponge, fill in the central square with a strong cobalt blue dye.

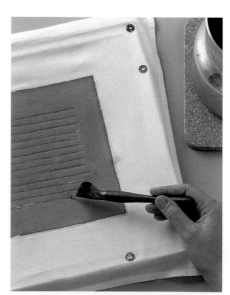

5 When the napkin is completely dry, wax in all the horizontal lines, about 1cm (¼ in) apart using a canting.

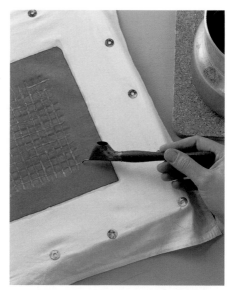

7 When the napkin is completely dry, wax in all the vertical lines using a canting.

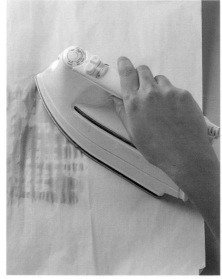

9 Leave the napkin to dry completely. Remove the napkin from the frame. Remove the wax by ironing between sheets of newsprint, brown or lining paper. Then dry-clean or boil the fabric, remembering to check first how the dye is fixed.

# COSMETIC BAG

To make the cosmetic bag water resistant, the wax was not fully removed from the batik and the bag was lined with a nylon splash-proof cloth similar to those used to make shower curtains. The marble effect was made by using the crackle technique.

1 Cut a piece of medium-weight cotton twice the size you have decided on for your finished washbag. Remember to include a 1 cm (½ in) seam allowance and wastage all round. Pin the cotton to a frame and cover the entire piece with molten wax.

2 Once the wax has set, remove the cloth from the frame and crumple it firmly between both hands. Small cracks should appear in the surface of the wax. Once the cloth has been "cracked" enough, smooth the cloth out flat and dampen.

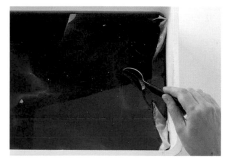

3 Prepare a navy blue dye bath according to the manufacturer's instructions. Place the damp batik in the bath for the recommended time, allowing the dye to penetrate the cracks in the wax.

4 Rinse the batik in cold water until the water runs clear, and leave to dry. Then, re-pin the cloth to the frame. Heat the wax with a hairdryer until molten. Allow the molten wax to seal up the cracks made in step 2.

5 When the wax has set, crumple the cloth again between your hands. Direct dye with a strong green dye and leave to dry. Rinse the batik until the water runs clear, then remove as much wax as possible with your fingers.

6 Iron out more of the wax by placing the batik between pieces of newsprint, brown or lining paper. Keep renewing the pieces of paper and ironing until the cloth has regained most of its flexibility, but still contains some wax. ▶

## MATERIALS AND EQUIPMENT YOU WILL NEED

Medium-weight cotton (sheeting) • Scissors • Silk pins • Frame • Crackle or general-purpose wax • Wax pot or double boiler • Large brush (for wax) • Dye: navy blue and green • Dye bath • Hairdryer • Iron • Newsprint, brown or lining paper • Pins • Sewing machine and thread • Needle • Nylon lining • White bias binding • Ribbon or cord

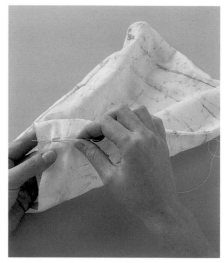

7 Cut the batik in half and cut the two pieces of lining cloth to the same dimensions. Pin, then sew up one side, leaving a 1 cm (½ in) gap 1 cm (½ in) down from the top. Iron this side seam flat and oversew round the 1 cm (½ in) hole to reinforce it. Sew the remaining side seam and the bottom to make a bag.

9 Open up a piece of bias binding long enough to run down the top of the bag. Line up the top edge of the bag with the reverse right edge of the binding. Pin, then stitch round the edge of the bag, using the crease on the bias binding as a guide.

10 Fold the bag right side out. Fold the bias binding on to the right side of the bag and topstitch, keeping as close to the edge of the binding as you can. Fold in the raw edge of the binding before sewing to keep it neat.

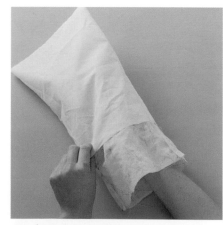

8 Take the two pieces of lining cloth and sew round three sides, leaving a 1 cm (½ in) seam allowance, to make another bag. Turn the batik bag inside out and place it inside the lining bag (right side out).

11 Sew two parallel lines of stitching to make a channel round the top of the bag to meet with the top and bottom of the gap in the side seam. Thread some ribbon or cord through the hole and along the channel. Pull up to close the bag.

# GREETING CARD

THIS CARD WAS MADE FROM GOOD QUALITY WRITING PAPER AND COLOURED WITH TRANSPARENT INKS. GREETING CARDS ARE AN EXCELLENT AND INVENTIVE WAY OF USING UP SCRAPS OF FABRIC OR PAPER. ALWAYS USE GOOD QUALITY PAPERS THAT WILL NOT BUCKLE WHEN WET WITH INK.

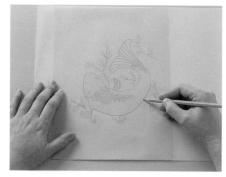

**1** Enlarge and trace the template design on to a piece of good quality coloured writing paper. Pin the paper to a frame.

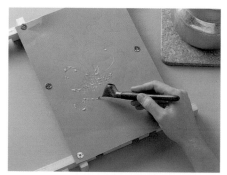

**2** Heat the wax. Using a canting, draw in the fish and scales with wax. The wax should stick firmly to the paper. If the wax brushes away easily, then it is not hot enough.

**3** Colour in the fish with blue ink, making sure that all the gaps around the scales have been filled in. Paint the background to the fish a light green. Always remember the effect the background colour will have when overpainting, for example, blue painted with light green will become sea green.

**4** Using a canting, fill in the seaweed shapes. Alternatively, you could use a brush to leave a different mark.

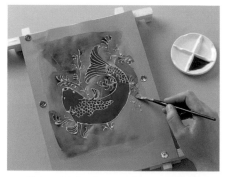

**5** Paint this background area with dark green ink. As it is impossible to wash away final grease marks, wax residue will remain on the card. To disguise these marks, paint the entire card with wax.

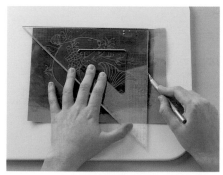

**6** Iron out as much wax as possible by placing the card between pieces of newsprint, brown or lining paper. Repeat this process until wax is no longer being absorbed. Trim down the design and mount it on a piece of folded card (card stock).

## MATERIALS AND EQUIPMENT YOU WILL NEED

TRACING PAPER • PENCIL • COLOURED WRITING PAPER • SILK PINS • FRAME • CANTING • GENERAL-PURPOSE WAX • WAX POT OR DOUBLE BOILER • INKS: BLUE, LIGHT GREEN AND DARK GREEN • PAINT BRUSHES (FOR INKS) • PAINT BRUSHES (FOR WAX) • IRON • NEWSPRINT, BROWN OR LINING PAPER • CRAFT KNIFE • SET (T) SQUARE • COLOURED CARD (CARD STOCK)

# SILK TIE

THIS READY-MADE SILK TIE WAS DECORATED BY THE SIMPLE USE OF A PIECE OF STRING DIPPED IN WAX. THIS IS A QUICK AND EASY WAY TO OBTAIN A STRAIGHT LINE. IRON-FIXED SILK PAINTS ARE USED, WHICH ARE THEN SET WHEN THE SILK IS IRONED AT THE END OF THE PROCESS.

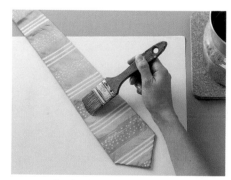

1 Place the tie on a plastic board. Heat the wax. Put a piece of string in the wax. Leave it until the wax has melted on the string. Pull it taut and then apply the wax on the string across the tie, according to the pattern.

2 Apply the wax in dots using the canting, following the pattern.

3 Paint or sponge on the pale blue silk paint. Turn over the tie and paint on the back. Blot with kitchen paper to absorb any excess dye. Leave to dry.

4 Apply the hot wax with a brush or sponge across the white spots, following the pattern.

5 Paint on the dark blue silk paint. Turn over the tie and paint on the back. Blot with kitchen paper to absorb any excess dye. Leave to dry.

6 Iron the tie between sheets of newsprint, brown or lining paper. Continue ironing with clean sheets of paper until no more wax appears. The heat will fix the dye. Have the tie dry-cleaned to remove the excess wax.

## MATERIALS AND EQUIPMENT YOU WILL NEED

WHITE READY-MADE SILK TIE • PLASTIC BOARD • STRING • GENERAL-PURPOSE WAX • WAX POT OR DOUBLE BOILER •
CANTING (MEDIUM SPOUT) • IRON-FIX SILK PAINTS: PALE BLUE, DARK BLUE • PAINTBRUSH OR SPONGE • KITCHEN PAPER (PAPER TOWEL) •
4 CM (1½ IN) WIDE BRUSH • IRON • NEWSPRINT, BROWN OR LINING PAPER

# TABLE RUNNER

THIS TABLE RUNNER WAS MADE FROM A DOUPION SILK AND DYED USING A MIXTURE OF DIRECT AND DYE BATH TECHNIQUES. THE FRAYED EDGE COULD BE EMBELLISHED WITH BEADS TO GIVE THE RUNNER A MORE ETHNIC FEEL OR HEMMED SQUARE FOR A MORE CONTEMPORARY LOOK.

**1** Cut a piece of doupion silk to the size you want for your table runner. Allow a 2 cm (¾ in) seam allowance all round and 2–4 cm (¾–1½ in) wastage. Enlarge and cut out the maple leaf shape on a piece of Mylar film or acetate using a craft knife.

**2** Pin the silk to a painting frame and, using the template, draw maple leaves randomly along the cloth. Place the leaves at different angles so that they look scattered rather than neatly placed.

**3** Heat the wax. Using a canting, apply wax around the outline of some of the leaves. Block in the remainder with a brush. Check the back of the fabric for breaks in the wax outline. Fill in any gaps by waxing on the back.

**4** Using a small brush, paint in with dye the leaves that were left with just a wax outline. Use autumn colours such as rusty browns or olive greens. ▶

## MATERIALS AND EQUIPMENT YOU WILL NEED

DOUPION SILK • SCISSORS • MYLAR FILM • CRAFT KNIFE • SILK PINS • FRAME • WATER-SOLUBLE DRESSMAKER'S PEN • CANTING • CRACKLE OR GENERAL-PURPOSE WAX • WAX POT OR DOUBLE BOILER • BRUSH (FOR WAX) • PAINTBRUSHES (FOR DYE) • AUTUMN-COLOURED DYE FOR DIRECT APPLICATION • BROWN DYE (FOR DYE BATH) • DYE BATH • IRON • NEWSPRINT, BROWN OR LINING PAPER • PIN • NEEDLE AND THREAD

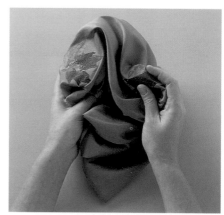

5 When the dyes have dried, block in the remaining leaves with wax. All the maple leaf shapes should now be solid wax. Remove the cloth from the frame and crumple the waxed leaves in your hands, cracking the surface of the wax.

7 When the cloth is dry, iron it between two pieces of newsprint, brown or lining paper until wax is no longer being absorbed. Have the fabric dry-cleaned to remove any grease marks and wax residue.

9 Trim away any wastage from both sides and iron a 1 cm (½ in) turnover. Then turn over another 1 cm (½ in) and iron again, giving a double turnover. Hemstitch this by hand.

6 Prepare a dye bath with a dark brown dye. The silk will have to be dry-cleaned to remove any wax residue, so make sure that the dye bath is made from a dye that is fast with dry-cleaning. Dampen the batik and place it in the dye bath, carefully following the dye manufacturer's instructions. When the cloth is the desired colour, remove it from the bath and rinse it under cool water until the water runs clear.

8 Using a pin, fray both ends of the batik. When fraying an edge, it is easier to pull a thread from across the whole width rather than allowing the threads to snap and pull out small sections, so go gently.

10 Divide the frayed edge at the top and bottom into equal sections and knot. Finally, trim the ends of the tassels so that they are nice and square.

# PAPER LAMPSHADE

THIS LAMPSHADE WAS MADE FROM A HAND-MADE JAPANESE PAPER WITH A STENCILLED BATIK DESIGN. HAND-MADE PAPERS WORK BEST IN THIS PROJECT, AS THEY ALLOW LIGHT TO PENETRATE MORE READILY, AND THE RICH TEXTURE OF THESE PAPERS GIVES A MORE NATURAL AND ORGANIC EFFECT.

1 Using a craft knife, cut away the old lampshade you are planning to replace and use this for your design pattern.

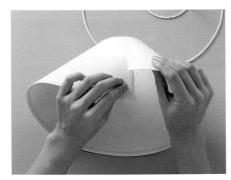

2 Create your template by drawing around the old shade on to a piece of tracing paper. Add 1 cm (½ in) to one straight edge. This is the template for the new shade. Cut out the template.

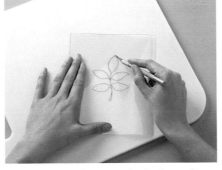

3 Enlarge and cut out the leaf template, not the stem from Mylar film using a craft knife. Plastic film is better than stencil card (card stock), as it allows you to peel off any hardened wax after use.

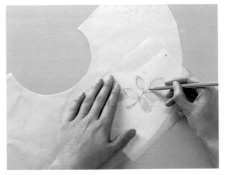

4 Map out your design by placing the stencil on the tracing paper template and drawing around the cut-out using a pencil. Repeat as often as you like. You can use this as a guide when working on the final shade.

5 Draw around the tracing paper design on to a piece of textured hand-made paper. Pin the paper to a frame.

6 Using your design as a guide, place the stencil on to the hand-made paper. Heat the wax. Fill the cut-out areas of the stencil with wax. To do this you can use a brush, rag, kitchen paper (paper towels) or cotton wool ball (cotton ball) clipped on to a clothes peg (pin). ▶

MATERIALS AND EQUIPMENT YOU WILL NEED

CRAFT KNIFE • OLD LAMPSHADE • TRACING PAPER • PENCIL • SCISSORS • MYLAR FILM • HAND-MADE PAPER • FRAME • GENERAL-PURPOSE WAX • WAX POT OR DOUBLE BOILER • BRUSH, RAG, KITCHEN PAPER (PAPER TOWELS) OR COTTON WOOL (BALLS) • CANTING • SPONGE BRUSH • BLUE INK • IRON • NEWSPRINT • DOUBLE-SIDED TAPE • NEEDLE • EMBROIDERY THREAD (FLOSS) TO MATCH FINAL SHADE COLOUR • CLOTHES PEG (PIN)

**7** Draw in all the leaf stems with molten wax using a canting.

**8** Using a sponge brush, paint the shade shape with blue ink. Wipe away any beads of ink that form on the waxed areas. Leave the shade to dry, then cover the entire shade shape with wax. It is necessary to do this as the paper cannot be washed and grease marks will be clearly visible unless the whole area is covered.

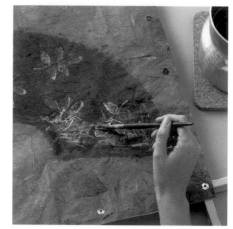

**9** Cut out the lampshade leaving about 1 cm (½ in) wastage at top and bottom. Iron out as much wax as possible by placing the shade between two sheets of newsprint, brown or lining paper. Keep renewing the paper until no more wax is being absorbed. If the papers get stuck together, heat the wax to molten and peel away the papers while still hot.

**10** Run a piece of narrow double-sided tape down the straight edge with the extra 1 cm (½ in). Bend the paper round and stick the straight edges together to form a cone.

**11** Cover the top and bottom rim of the light fitting with double-sided tape. Turn the paper cone upside down and place the light fitting inside, pressing the sticky top rim into the top of the paper cone. Drop the sticky bottom ring into the cone, allowing the paper to stick to the ring. Cut and fold in the 1 cm (½ in) paper wastage at the top and bottom of the cone to cover the metal ring.

**12** Sew around the top and bottom rings with embroidery thread (floss) so that the thread is wrapped round them. This will help secure the paper to the rings.

# LEATHER BOOK COVER

THIS BOOK COVER IS MADE FROM NATURAL COLOURED LEATHER AND DECORATED WITH YELLOW, RED, GREEN AND BLACK DYES. THE CRACKING EFFECT IS DISTINCTIVE OF BATIK DYEING, AND IS ACHIEVED BY CRUMPLING THE LEATHER VERY GENTLY TO CRACK THE WAX AND LET THE DYE SEEP IN.

**1** Enlarge and trace the template on to tracing paper. Dampen the leather with a piece of cotton wool (cotton ball) dipped in water, then transfer the design from the paper on to the leather.

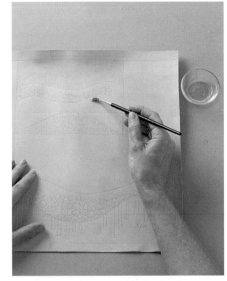

**2** Cut out the piece for the book cover from the leather with a craft knife. Work on a cutting mat to protect the underlying surface. Allow the leather to dry completely before using the gum. Brush the gum over the leather on those areas you want to remain white (or natural leather colour).

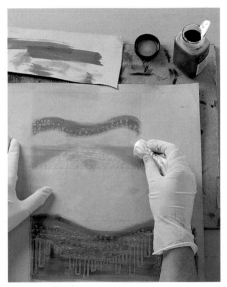

**3** Wear latex gloves when using leather dyes. Dip a wool dauber or cotton wool into the yellow dye. Press the pad on to a scrap of leather to remove any excess dye and then, beginning in one corner, move the pad from left to right over the surface of the leather book cover. Do this with the green dye too. ▶

## MATERIALS AND EQUIPMENT YOU WILL NEED
TRACING PAPER • PENCIL • NATURAL LEATHER • COTTON WOOL • CRAFT KNIFE • CUTTING MAT • BRUSH • GUM • LATEX GLOVES •
WOOL DAUBER • LEATHER DYE: YELLOW, RED, GREEN AND BLACK • SOFT CLOTH • BOARD • METAL RULER • SPRAY ADHESIVE • MOUNT BOARD •
LEATHER LACQUER SPRAY • DECORATIVE PAPER

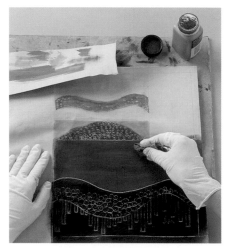

4 Once the whole area has been coated, leave it to dry naturally. When dry, cover the yellow part of the design with gum and the areas that are to remain green. Apply red dye on the leather with a cotton wool pad. When completely dry, again block out those areas that are to remain red.

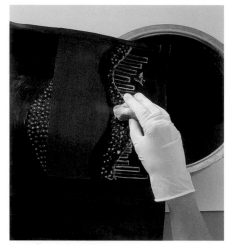

6 Place the leather on a board and remove the gum with a large piece of damp cotton wool. Wash thoroughly with plenty of cold water.

8 When the leather is completely dry, apply a coat of spray adhesive on the reverse side of the leather. Place a piece of mount board over the top and press the pieces together firmly to stick.

5 You are now ready to dye the leather black. However, before using the black dye, crumple the leather well to achieve a good "crackled" effect on the surface, which is the distinctive characteristic of batik dying.

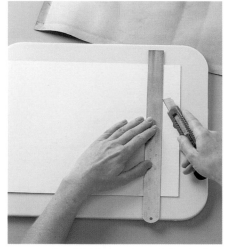

7 Bend and fold the edges of the leather while it is still damp, to form its proper shape. Mitre the corners so the leather folds easily.

9 Clean the leather and spray with lacquer to protect the leather. Finish the inside surface by covering it with decorative paper of your choice.

# BATIK SCREEN

SCREENS ARE USED AS ROOM DIVIDERS THOUGH THEY CAN BE USED TO DIFFUSE OR SOFTEN LIGHT FROM A WINDOW. WHEN YOU WANT LIGHT TO SHINE THROUGH THE SCREEN, REMEMBER TO USE LIGHTWEIGHT CLOTH AND LIGHT-FAST DYES. SCREENS ARE MADE BY HINGING TOGETHER A SERIES OF FRAMES.

1 Measure the inside edge of your screen's frame. Add at least 3 cm (1¼ in) wastage all around. If you are using a plainweave cloth rather than a satin or twill, you can tear the cloth down to size which will ensure a straight line.

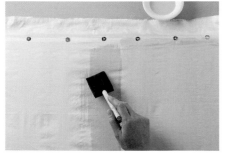

2 Pin the silk to the frame. Divide the length of silk roughly in half between two contrasting colours such as lilac and lime green. Apply the dye quickly using a sponge brush or soft kitchen brush. If you are using an iron-fix dye, dry the cloth with a hairdryer to fix the dye.

3 Heat the wax. In the top quarter of the cloth, draw lines of wax across the fabric using a canting. It is not necessary to have totally straight lines as slight curves or wobbles will create more of a pattern.

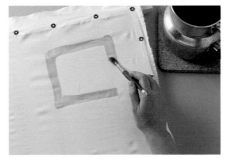

4 In the bottom quarter of the cloth, draw a square with wax using a medium-sized brush. To create a more interesting finished piece, use a variety of tools when waxing as this will vary the types of mark in the cloth.

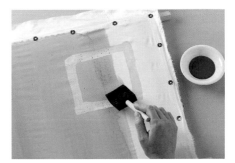

5 Over-paint the entire piece of cloth with a pale blue. Beads of dye that form on the surface of waxed areas should be removed as dye does sometimes penetrate the wax after long periods. These spots can, however, add texture to a design so you may wish to leave them.

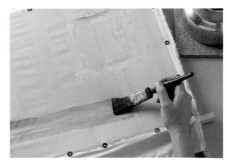

6 Allow the blue dye to dry. If you are using a hairdryer, make sure the cloth does not become so hot as to turn the applied wax molten. Paint a stripe of wax down one side of the cloth using a coarse household brush. ▶

### MATERIALS AND EQUIPMENT YOU WILL NEED

WOODEN SCREEN • TAPE MEASURE • LIGHTWEIGHT SILK • SILK PINS • FRAME • HEAT-FIXED DYES: LILAC, LIME GREEN, PALE BLUE • SPONGE BRUSH OR KITCHEN BRUSH • HAIRDRYER (OPTIONAL) • WAX • WAX POT OR DOUBLE BOILER • CANTING • MEDIUM-SIZED BRUSH • SALT • IRON • NEWSPRINT, BROWN OR LINING PAPER • DOUBLE-SIDED TAPE • STAPLE GUN • SCISSORS • MASKING TAPE • FABRIC GLUE • RIBBON OR BRAID

**7** Over-paint again and add more stripes or squares. Salt can be applied to damp dye to create texture. You will see that the salt draws the dye towards it creating dark lines and spots. The cloth must be completely dry before the salt is removed.

**8** Remove the cloth from the frame and remove the wax by ironing between sheets of newsprint, brown or lining paper, and dry-cleaning. Then prepare the remaining pieces of cloth for each frame of your screen. On the first panel of your screen run a strip of narrow double-sided tape around the inside edge of the frame (on the face of the screen).

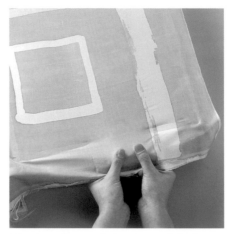

**9** Stretch one of the pieces of cloth across the frame, sticking it to the double-sided tape. Pull the cloth tight, making sure there are no wrinkles and that the cloth is springy to the touch. The cloth can be pulled up from the double-sided tape and re-stuck when adjustments need to be made.

**10** Staple the edges of the cloth to the frame. Place staples an equal distance apart along the area that was covered by double-sided tape.

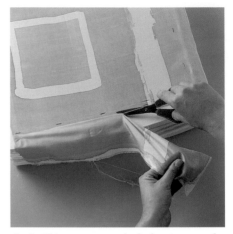

**11** Trim away any cloth that is unstuck using a pair of sharp scissors. Cover the raw edges with masking tape to prevent any fraying.

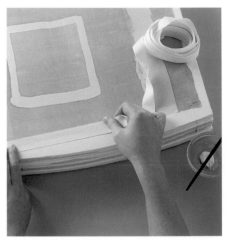

**12** Using strong fabric glue or clear drying adhesive, cover the untidy topside edges with ribbon or braid. Repeat steps 9 to 12 to cover all the remaining frames that make up the screen.

# TIGER DECKCHAIR

USE BATIK DYEING TO TRANSFORM AN OLD OR STANDARD DECKCHAIR INTO A UNIQUE AND EYE-CATCHING CENTREPIECE OF ANY GARDEN, DECK OR CONSERVATORY. THIS TIGER MOTIF IS CERTAINLY STUNNING, BUT YOU CAN USE YOUR OWN DESIGN, IF YOU PREFER.

1 Remove the seat from an old deckchair and use this as a template for the new cover. Add an additional 2 cm (¾ in) all around for seam allowance and wastage. Remember to use a cloth strong enough to take a person's weight, such as heavy canvas.

2 Enlarge and trace the design on to the cloth. Continue the stripes until the entire cloth has been covered. Pin the cloth to the frame. Making sure the cloth is stretched really taut.

3 Heat the wax. Using a canting, wax the outline of the tiger's head, paws, eyebrows and the irises of the eyes. As this project uses a heavy cloth, you may find that the wax does not completely penetrate the cloth. You can fill in the breaks in the wax by waxing on the back. However, allowing the dyes to bleed into one another does add a more loose and painterly effect such as has been achieved here.

## MATERIALS AND EQUIPMENT YOU WILL NEED

DECKCHAIR • TRACING PAPER • PENCIL • SILK PINS • LINEN (HEAVYWEIGHT) • FRAME • CANTING • GENERAL-PURPOSE WAX •
WAX POT OR DOUBLE BOILER • BRUSHES (FOR WAX) • DYES (FOR DIRECT DYEING METHOD) • SOFT BRUSHES (FOR DYE) •
SPONGE BRUSH OR KITCHEN SPONGE • HAIRDRYER • IRON • NEWSPRINT, BROWN OR LINING PAPER • SCISSORS • PINS •
SEWING MACHINE AND THREAD • UPHOLSTERY PINS AND HAMMER

4 Using a canting and/or brush, block in with wax the claws and whites of the tiger's eyes.

5 Fill in the tiger's iris with olive green dye and the eyebrows with a dark brown dye. Using a larger brush, fill in the background to the tiger with dark brown dye (the bottom of the cloth on the finished chair).

6 Fill in the colours for the tiger, fading the colours from a pale orange at the tiger's head to a strong cherry red at the other end of the cloth. When blending colours, it is important to work quickly so that the colours bleed into each other while still wet. To help with quick coverage, use a large sponge brush or soft kitchen sponge.

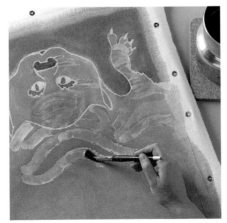

7 If you are using an iron-fix dye, use a hairdryer to help dry the cloth. This will also help fix the dye. When the cloth is completely dry, use a brush to wax the outline to the tiger stripes. Use a thicker brush when you are about halfway down the cloth. Do not worry about breaks in the wax outline.

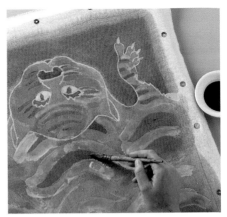

8 Paint in the stripes with a dark brown dye. Allow the dyes to bleed from breaks in the waxed outlines. This will give a more textured effect to the stripes.

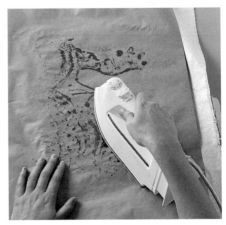

9 Remove the batik from the frame and pick off as much wax as possible with your fingers. Iron out the wax by placing the cloth between sheets of newsprint, brown or lining paper. To remove final wax remnants, have the batik dry-cleaned. Trim down the batik to the correct size for your seat.  ▶

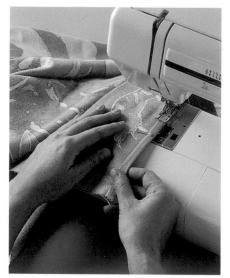

**10** Iron and pin a double 1 cm (½ in) turnover down both sides of the fabric and sew with a medium zigzag stitch using a sewing machine. It is important to use zigzag rather than running stitch, as this will allow the fabric to stretch without snapping.

**12** Nail the seat on to the chair frame using upholstery pins. Start with the central pin, then the pins at either end. Space the remainder of the pins evenly; there should be no more than 2.5 cm (1 in) between each pin.

**11** Turn over the top and bottom 2 cm (¾ in) seam allowance and machine sew, again with a zigzag stitch.

# Templates

The Measurements for each template are those used within the individual projects. Where no measurements are given, they are reproduced at the same size, or an enlargement size is specified. For an enlargement, either use a grid system or photocopier.

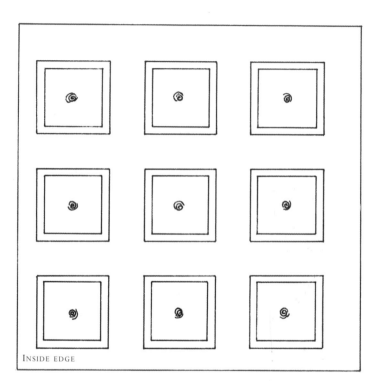

Inside edge

Silk Square Square Scarf pp30–32
Enlarge by 400% to 15 x 15 in (37.5 x 37.5 cm) for exact size

Tiger Deckchair pp86–9
Enlarge by 500% for exact size

Pastel Blind pp36–8
Enlarge by 200% for exact size

GREETING CARD pp70–1
ENLARGE BY 200%

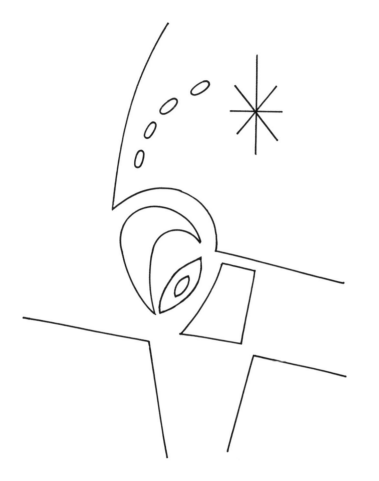

ABSTRACT PICTURE pp33–5
ENLARGE BY 400% FOR EXACT SIZE

TABLE RUNNER pp74–6
ENLARGE BY 200% FOR EXACT SIZE

SHAWL PP42–4
ENLARGE BY 200% FOR EXACT SIZE

LEATHER BOOKMARK PP58–60
ENLARGE BY 120% FOR EXACT SIZE

PICTURE FRAME PP45–7
ENLARGE BY 200% FOR EXACT SIZE

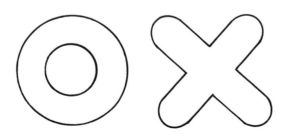

COTTON SARONG PP52–4
ENLARGE BY 200% FOR EXACT SIZE

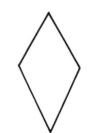

SILK VELVET MUFFLER PP55–7
ENLARGE BY 200% FOR EXACT SIZE

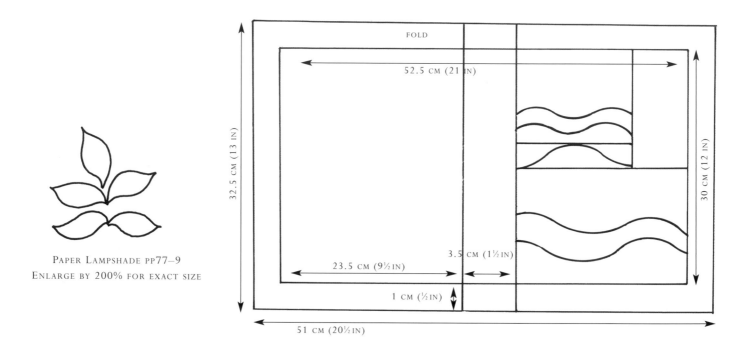

PAPER LAMPSHADE PP77–9
ENLARGE BY 200% FOR EXACT SIZE

FOLD

52.5 CM (21 IN)

32.5 CM (13 IN)

30 CM (12 IN)

3.5 CM (1½ IN)

23.5 CM (9½ IN)

1 CM (½ IN)

51 CM (20½ IN)

LEATHER BOOK COVER PP80–2

TABLE MATS PP39–41
ENLARGE BY 250% FOR EXACT SIZE

# SUPPLIERS & ACKNOWLEDGEMENTS

The publishers would like to thank the following artists for the beautiful projects photographed in this book:

Helen Heery for the Silk Square Scarf pp30–2, Abstract Picture pp 33–5, Cotton Sarong pp 52–4, Silk Velvet Muffler pp 55–57 and the Silk Tie pp 72–3. Sipra Majumder for the Leather Bookmark pp 58–60 and Leather Book Cover pp 80–2. All other projects made by the author.

**UK SUPPLIERS**
Pongees
28-30 Hoxton Square
London N1 6NN
*Silk specialists.*

Poth Hille & Co. Ltd.
37 High Street
Stratford
London E15 2QD
*Suppliers of waxes.*

Suasion Ltd.
35 Riding House Street
London W1P 7PT
*Suppliers of fabric, equipment and materials.*

George Weil & Sons Ltd.
(Mail order)
The Warehouse
Reading Arch Road
Redhill
Surrey
*Suppliers of fabric, equipment and materials.*

**US SUPPLIERS**
Dick Blick Art Materials
P.O.Box 1267
695 US Highway 150 East
Galesburg, IL 61402
www.dickblick.com

Earth Guild
33 Haywood Street
Asheville, NC 28801
Tel: (828) 255-7818
Fax: (828) 255-8593
www.earthguild.com

Dharma Trading Co.
P.O. Box 150916
San Rafael, CA 94915
Tel: (415) 456-7657
Fax: (415) 456-8747
www.dharmatrading.com

Jerry's Artarama
P.O. Box 58638
Raleigh, NC 27658
Tel: (800) 827-8478

North End Fabrics
31 Harrison Avenue
Boston, MA 02111
Tel: (617) 542-2763

The publishers would like to thank all the contributors to the gallery: Alison Tilley, Helen Heery, Rosi Robinson, Hetty van Boekhout, Sipra Majumder, Heather Gatt and especially to Noel Dyrenforth for kindly allowing us to photograph his work.

**Picture credits**
The publishers would like to thank the following agencies for permission to reproduce pictures in this book:

Pages 8, 9t, 11bl – Victoria and Albert Museum Picture Library. Page 9br – James Davis Travel Photography. Page 10tl – John Wender; Eye Ubiquitous. Pages 10br, 11tr – The Bridgeman Art Library.

# INDEX